Adaptable Interventions for Counseling Concerns

Adaptable Interventions for Counseling Concerns is filled with more than 40 interventions appropriate for new and experienced professionals alike. The interventions are organized in a unique yet practical manner, including options for individual reader creativity and personal adaptations within the text itself. The book's uniqueness lies in the broad coverage of common concerns, formatting, and ease in navigation. Each chapter is devoted to a specific client concern, with seven suggested intervention strategies clearly labeled by modality to make it easy for readers to find new interventions best suited to their practice. Chapters also introduce relevant and recent research on client concerns, contextualizing the circumstances for which a counseling professional could apply the chosen interventions. Intervention sections also include space for individualized notes and reader personalization.

Freeman Woolnough, MEd, CCC, is a counselor who supports post-secondary students in Ontario. Outside of the counseling office, he delivers workshops and presentations across Canada on a variety of mental health topics.

Autumn Marie Chilcote, MEd, is a psychological services professional specializing in person-centered and creative therapies. She provides counseling, research, and education across a range of public and private industries.

Adaptable Interventions for Counseling Concerns

A Step-by-Step Clinical Workbook

Freeman Woolnough
Autumn Marie Chilcote

Routledge
Taylor & Francis Group
NEW YORK AND LONDON

First published 2017
by Routledge
605 Third Avenue, New York, NY 10017

and by Routledge
2 Park Square, Milton Park, Abingdon, Oxon, OX14 4RN

Routledge is an imprint of the Taylor & Francis Group, an informa business

Library of Congress Cataloging in Publication Data
Names: Woolnough, Freeman, author. | Chilcote, Autumn Marie, author.
Title: Adaptable interventions for counseling concerns : a step-by-step clinical workbook / by Freeman Woolnough, Autumn Marie Chilcote.
Description: New York, NY : Routledge, 2017. | Includes bibliographical references and index.
Identifiers: LCCN 2016027081 | ISBN 9781138644144 (hardback : alk. paper) | ISBN 9781138644151 (pbk. : alk. paper) | ISBN 9781315622200 (ebook)
Subjects: LCSH: Counseling psychology. | Motivational interviewing. | Clinical psychology.
Classification: LCC BF636.6 .W665 2017 | DDC 158.3—dc23
LC record available at https://lccn.loc.gov/2016027081

ISBN: 978-1-138-64414-4 (hbk)
ISBN: 978-1-138-64415-1 (pbk)
ISBN: 978-1-315-62220-0 (ebk)

Typeset in Warnock Pro
by Apex CoVantage, LLC

We would like to dedicate this book to all of the helping professionals within the counseling and therapy community of practice. It is your openness to creativity that inspires clients toward change.

Contents

Acknowledgments

Many of the ideas underlying *Adaptable Interventions* began in a small city called Prince George, in British Columbia (Canada). We would like to thank our graduate cohort, supervisors, community, and many friends whose creativity and inspiring attitudes allowed us to grow as both people and counselors. Without all of you, this book certainly would not exist.

Throughout the writing process, a number of individuals have helped to support us. Thanks to Benjamin Chilcote for being an amazing friend and partner. Thank you Jonathan Amanatidis, Ethan Harper, Nora Harper, Lucretia Kelleher, Michael Kelleher, Nichole Kelleher, Carmen Law, Jerome Pressley, Nathan Riley, Molly Raffan, Nadia Sawaya Fehr, and Julie Williams, all of whom, along with Benjamin, were involved in the photos throughout this book. A special shout-out to Olivia Kelleher, who was doing all the hard work while we took the photos.

We are very much in gratitude to the editorial, copy editing, typesetting, and production staff at Routledge. In particular, we would like to thank Anna Moore and Zoey Peresman, who have worked with us from day one to get this project off the ground.

Finally, we would like to acknowledge and thank public libraries. While they are always at risk of closure due to ever-changing technologies and budgets, they continue to provide free and comprehensive access to knowledge and ideas from across the globe. Thank you for inspiring us.

Introduction

There is not, nor should there ever be, counseling or therapy that consists solely of interventions and techniques. Counseling sessions that rely primarily on techniques will always pale in comparison to those that focus on the client-professional relationship. For this reason, most counseling and therapy training programs will (rightfully) focus on developing soft skills as the building blocks for helping professionals. However, interventions are still a vital part of the therapeutic process, especially in its early stages; how to navigate the transformation of the client's experience sometimes falls to the words we say and perspectives that can come from unique, intervention-based activities. Eventually, through using specific interventions and strategies, the counseling process develops into a natural, comfortable rhythm that is less 'step-by-step' and more ingrained or instinctive. This development requires time, experience, and frameworks from which to grow.

These frameworks are particularly useful for newer helping professionals, coming from a place of caring and excitement, and possessing many skills but few specific intervention strategies. Because of this, new helping professionals, while feeling confident in their skillset and knowledge, may still find themselves occasionally at a loss in-session. In the initial years following formal training, it is common to latch onto and attempt to use a variety of different interventions and frameworks to decide what works best for the individual professional.

Additionally, more experienced helping professionals may develop 'intervention fatigue' through a number of years of using the same frameworks and interventions. Boredom and waning interest can arise from falling into the habit of using the same interventions or activities for the more common issues seen in their offices. Seeking out new interventions that can effectively be adapted to fit individual beliefs can ease this fatigue and revitalize interest in the counseling field.

The intent behind *Adaptable Interventions for Common Counseling Concerns* is to provide intervention frameworks to helping professionals working with a number of common client concerns. *Adaptable Interventions* offers a number of new and effective interventions that will spark novel ideas for both new and experienced helping professionals.

The core content of the following pages consists of over 45 counseling interventions, each developed with unique intents and goals for working with clients. In no way are the authors suggesting that helping professionals discard all current interventions and use only those found in this book. Rather, use these interventions to supplement and enhance your current practices, enriching the counseling experience for both client and professional.

It is important to note that research in the field consistently points to evidence that it is neither the words that are said, nor the frameworks that are used, but rather the relationship that the helping professional has with their client, that will determine the outcome of counseling (Lambert & Barley, 2001). With this in mind, the interventions found within this book have been developed with the intent of adaptability; take the words, questions, and actions from the individual interventions and make them fit for your own unique therapeutic relationships. Many of these interventions may trigger a sense of familiarity for some professionals, as the authors' backgrounds and processes are derived from many traditional and evidence-based counseling frameworks. However, each intervention has been uniquely developed for the purposes of sparking new and novel ideas for helping professionals, drawing on the in-session counseling experience of the authors.

Though intervention books are not rare, the uniqueness of *Adaptable Interventions* lies in its formatting and ease of navigation. The interventions found within, while certainly not exhaustive, address a number of counseling concerns across a wide breadth of topics that are of interest to helping professionals across the board.

▶ REFERENCE

Lambert, M. J. & Barley, D. E. (2001). Research summary on the therapeutic relationship and psychotherapy outcome. *Psychotherapy: Theory, Research, Practice, Training, 38*(4), 357–361. http://dx.doi.org/10.1037/0033-3204.38.4.357 Retrieved February 15th, 2016.

▶ HOW TO USE THIS BOOK

Adaptable Interventions for Counseling Concerns is designed with the reader in mind, using an easy-to-access layout and structure. Here is what you will find in the following pages:

Chapters Each of the first six chapters is devoted to a general client concern. These concerns have been included because of the frequency and relatively common presenting issues that are seen in offices of helping professionals. For more information about the relevancy of the particular topics, as well as the rationale of what is and what is not included in this book, please see page xviii. The final chapter, 'Endings,' provides context and interventions for therapeutic relationships which are transitioning or coming to a close.

A Note About the Chapter Introductions . . .

Each chapter begins with a short introduction to the topic at hand. These introductions expand upon the definitions and terms associated with the topic, clarifying for the reader how the authors interpret the particular counseling concern. The terms are framed around common phrases that helping professionals may hear when working with clients who are seeking support for these concerns. There is also a brief summary of research around each topic. Note that this summary is not meant to be comprehensive, but has been included for reference and context.

Interventions All of the interventions found within are applicable for teens and adults, and the majority of them are adaptable to a younger client population. There are seven interventions in each chapter, one each of the following types:

Psychoeducational

Interventions which serve to educate the client on certain aspects of biology, psychology, or society, with the intent of enhancing the client's understanding of their current concern.

Talk-Based/Motivational

Interventions that primarily consist of discussion and dialogue between the client and helping professional, often useful when the client is having difficulties shifting perspectives within the session.

Art-Based

Interventions that involve drawing, painting, or other forms of visual arts. It is important to recognize that art-based interventions are focused on the process, not the product.

Hands-On

Interventions that break from more traditional, talk-based activities. Hands-on interventions tend to involve some level of physicality, though note that most do not require a large range of motion.

Relational

Interventions which turn the focus to clients in relation to themselves, often involving an added level of introspection.

Group

Interventions that are directed toward participants in a group setting, where the group ideally consists of five to 12 participants.

Homework

Interventions which are completed by the client on their own time, between sessions. Homework interventions also include debriefs for when the client returns. Note that due to the nature of the topic, the 'Endings' chapter does not include a homework intervention.

Each Intervention is Divided Into the Following Sections

Amount of Time

How long to expect the intervention to take. Note that for homework interventions, the times for the explanation of the homework as well as the follow-up debriefs are both included.

Materials Needed

A list of suggested materials, which can be very useful when preparing sessions in advance.

Intent/Used for . . .

A brief description of under what circumstances this intervention may be useful. These are only suggestions, as the interventions in this book can be adapted to serve multiple purposes.

Step-by-Step Instructions

From start to finish, the 'basics' of how to go about approaching the intervention.

Guiding Questions

A list of questions and phrases that can be useful in moving the intervention along or eliciting the sharing of thoughts and feelings from clients.

Tips/Ways to Change

This section suggests some (not all) alternative ways to adapt the intervention. Adaptations for different age groups as well as considerations for various populations are included for many interventions.

Notes

Each intervention includes some blank space at the end, which can be used for your own adaptations and notes about using the intervention.

Additional Sections

At the end of the book, you will find two Afterwords, both of which can be useful for helping professionals in a variety of contexts:

Hope-Work

A series of quick, homework-based activities that can be given to clients across the board, often regardless of their counseling concerns.

Words We Like

Questions and phrases that are applicable in nearly any counseling situation, drawn from the authors' training and experience.

▶ A NOTE ABOUT THE TOPICS

There are an extraordinary number of counseling concerns that can be addressed in a text such as this, as the diversity of presenting issues is as diverse as the clients that we encounter. The main topics that have been presented in these pages represent consideration of the experiences of the authors as well as open discussions with professional peers. When asked about common counseling concerns that arise on a daily basis, many counseling professionals answer similarly: anxiety or depression, managing emotions, challenges with relationships, career or meaning-making (herein titled Identity), the need for trauma-informed approaches, and finally, termination or ending the counseling process. These concerns are represented across a broad spectrum, from discomfort and frustration to life-disruption and even clinical diagnoses. And while the symptoms, frequency, and intensity may vary, the authors consider these general counseling concerns to be those that are most often presented by clients, and most often require creative and practical approaches. Further, relief from the intensity of these general counseling concerns has proven to be helpful with clients presenting a range of more specific and unique issues or symptoms.

There are a number of concerns that are not included in this text; many of these are better addressed more comprehensively in other works. Concerns associated with grief and loss, and symptoms and pathologies resulting in other clinical concerns such as substance misuse, disordered eating, self-harming behaviors, and suicidality deserve a full text. Much has been written on these, and other, complex presenting concerns. The authors hope that readers will seek additional resources for these concerns, and also find the approaches detailed here adaptable to some of the symptoms of these more complex clinical concerns.

1 Stress and Anxiety

▶ WHAT ARE *STRESS AND ANXIETY* CONCERNS?

Feelings of stress, as well as the varied accompanying effects, contribute to some of the most common issues for which clients seek help (Guindon, 2011). It is important to note that this prevalence comes as no surprise; the stress reaction itself is a natural part of the human experience, and is one of the most common reactions in nature. At low to moderate levels, stress can actually be quite beneficial (McGonigal, 2015), and in many ways has contributed to our survival as a species. Unfortunately for many, stress has a contradictory nature. When experienced at high levels or for prolonged periods of time, stress and anxiety can significantly and negatively impact day-to-day tasks. These effects are typically what will bring clients into our offices for support. Below are some examples of what clients may say when looking for support around stress or anxiety.

"I've been unable to concentrate recently; my focus is wandering all over the place."

The stress reaction at the physiological level is often referred to as the *fight-or-flight* reaction (McEwan, 2005). At its most basic level, stress is triggered by a threat to the person; the trigger itself can be physical or psychological. In preparation for dealing with this threat, the person's attention is drawn to the trigger. From a survival standpoint this makes sense, given that we need to be aware of what is happening around us in order to keep ourselves safe. For clients who are experiencing stress or anxiety concerns, however, this focus on the threat can often lead to an inability to concentrate on other areas of their lives. Note that a lack of concentration can also be indicative of other mental health concerns (American Psychiatric Association, 2013), though it is commonly mentioned by clients who are experiencing difficulties with stress or anxiety.

"I haven't been able to get to sleep recently—my thoughts are keeping me awake."

The terms stress and anxiety are used almost interchangeably in today's society. Though they are, in fact, two aspects of the same physiological reaction, the terms refer to different psychological notions. For the purposes of this chapter, *stress* refers to an occurring fight-or-flight reaction that matches the triggering threat. For example, when faced with an exam in the first semester of university, most students feel a certain level of heightened awareness and difficulty in calming oneself until after the exam has finished. This reaction is expected, and proves to be useful at moderate levels, as the racing thoughts can contribute to planning for success (McGonigal, 2015). One common side effect of stress is sleeplessness; in particular, clients may find getting to sleep can be difficult because of their body's natural inclination toward focusing and concentrating on threats.

"Everybody tells me that I'm overreacting and stressing out over small things."

On the other hand, *anxiety* refers to a fight-or-flight reaction that is mismatched, or above and beyond the reaction that is typically expected from a certain triggering threat. In the above example of a student facing their first university exam, if the student is experiencing sleeplessness and thoughts about exam failure three months before the exam is scheduled to take place, we would typically consider this reaction to be anxiety. In these cases, it is important that helping professionals recognize that the underlying physiological reaction is the same for both stress and anxiety; the differences lie within the intensity. For this reason, the intent in helping clients with stress or anxiety concerns is to manage or regulate the reaction. Because it is an essential biological process, it would be difficult (and possibly harmful) to eliminate it entirely.

"I've been having a lot of anxiety . . ."

As noted earlier, it has become commonplace for the general population to interchange the terms stress and anxiety. In part due to the prevalence of stress-related issues, there is also a growing knowledge of mental health diagnoses and supports, although this knowledge can be limited in the general public (Furnham & Lousley, 2013). While this phenomenon can positively impact a client's decision to seek out help, we recently have seen an increase in the number of clients coming to our offices having already self-diagnosed with 'anxiety.' Though many of these clients may indeed already have a diagnosis, or may fit the criteria, it is essential that helping professionals are aware of the diagnostic criteria for *Generalized Anxiety Disorder* (*GAD*), found in the *Diagnostic and Statistical Manual of Mental Disorders* (American Psychiatric Association, 2013). While it is not in all helping professionals' frameworks or professional capabilities to actually diagnose a client, some may find it useful mentioning the distinction between GAD and other stress-related issues, and should consider consulting with a clinical or medical health professional.

"It felt like I couldn't breathe—was I having a heart attack?"

Some clients may present with stress that exists seemingly with no apparent threat or trigger. When the fight-or-flight reaction occurs in this scenario, or if a person is having a reaction to the possibility of a reaction—anxiety about anxiety—in this text, this is referred to as *panic*. Another part of the stress reaction is the escape response, which triggers increased breathing and pulse rates, as well as increased muscle tension. These symptoms, in particular, are exacerbated during panic, and clients can feel overwhelmed, sometimes with a sense of dread. Though stress, anxiety, and panic all have the potential to arise for intense, specific periods of time (attacks), panic in particular seems most likely to present in attack form (Bourne, 2010). Assuring clients that the reaction itself is not deadly can be an integral part of therapy.

"I just don't know what to do."

Sometimes a client may present with underlying indicators of stress, but with an additional symptom: an inability to make a decision or choice. This phenomenon is sometimes referred to as *choice paralysis*. A relatively newer concept, choice paralysis is indeed linked to the fight-or-flight response—scientists have shown that the response can actually contain a third component, a freeze response (Bracha, Ralston, Matsukawa, Williams, & Bracha, 2004). With this in mind, choice paralysis is simply another way that our bodies react to stress, and any of the interventions found in this chapter may therefore be useful in helping clients to address this concern.

▶ RELEVANCE

As noted above, the stress (fight-or-flight) response is one of the most natural reactions in the human body. When triggered at the appropriate level, stress can help our brains and bodies deal with threats, manage problems, and focus just enough to meet our goals. Countless studies have shown that an appropriate level of stress can be beneficial for performance on a number of tasks, including test-taking and project completion (McGonigal, 2015). In fact, people who are experiencing little to no stress will typically perform sub-par on a variety of tasks, showing that stress is a necessary part of the human experience.

On the other hand, the ideal level of stress is not limitless; people with higher levels of ongoing stress, anxiety, or panic will also perform sub-par. Because stress is a very natural reaction, it should come as no surprise that stress and anxiety issues make up more than 40% of client concerns in some therapeutic settings (American Psychological Association, 2013). Despite stress being a beneficial reaction, it is important to recognize that the stress response excels when dealing with physical threats—and in today's world, the vast majority of threats and triggers are psychological in nature (worry about the future, concern about relationships, etc.). The human population in general, and clients specifically, tend to fall on the distress/over-stress end of the spectrum, and providing them with stress-management and anxiety-reduction techniques and strategies generally proves to be quite useful, regardless of the trigger.

▶ WHAT WORKS WELL

Outside of the psychological or therapeutic setting, clients will often seek out medical support, and therefore it is integral that helping professionals are aware that medication is an option to help manage stress and anxiety. Although medication has had limited success when used as the sole treatment option (Kimmel, Roy-Byrne, & Cowley, 2015), many clients still see benefit if other treatments are not amenable. Typical anxiety management medication falls into two categories. Longer-term treatment medications, such as selective serotonin re-uptake inhibitors (SSRIs), are more commonly prescribed, and are thought to help with cases where anxiety is underlying or pervasive across all areas of a person's life. Shorter-term medications, such as benzodiazepines, can also be prescribed for anxiety or panic attacks, and can be effective for in-the-moment stress management (Kimmel et al., 2015). Of course, as with all medications, there are side effects, and the risk of dependence is very real; close consultation with a clinical or medical health professional is critical should concerns arise from medication usage.

As with medication, we would be amiss to omit the importance of healthy lifestyles when working with stress and anxiety issues. Both caffeine and nicotine have been shown to exacerbate the symptoms of the stress response; therefore, it is generally recommended that clients reduce coffee and cigarette use (Crocq, 2003). Increasing the association between positive health and physical distress, such as a racing heart and perspiration, can also be beneficial. Ensuring that clients are getting regular physical activity in their schedules is also a recommended first step to stress reduction.

Cognitive Behavioral Therapy (CBT) is a popular therapeutic framework used by many helping professionals for mental health concerns across the board. Though initially developed for working with low mood and depression (see the Low Mood and Depression chapter on page 33), CBT has also been shown to be effective for stress and anxiety concerns. This is not surprising, as some anxiety concerns tend to be cognition-based, the target of CBT-based interventions.

Mindfulness and acceptance-based approaches to symptom reduction, focusing on present awareness, nonjudgment, and acceptance, prove promising in reducing symptoms of stress and generalized anxiety. Dialectical Behavior Therapy (DBT) encourages mindful awareness of emotions, and exploring ways that emotional awareness can influence intentional behaviors and relationships. Acceptance and Commitment Therapy, integrating mindful awareness and elements of motivational interviewing, shows benefits for those managing stress and anxiety-related impulse control. Mindfulness-Based Stress Reduction, focusing on cognitive awareness and nonjudgment, also includes elements of reduction of physiological symptoms of stress and anxiety, such as sensory perception and physical tension (Baer, 2006). Mindfulness-based approaches are both skill- and knowledge-based, with applications for individual and group settings.

▶ FUTURE RESEARCH

There is a lack of research on the usefulness and effectiveness of therapeutic approaches for stress and anxiety reduction beyond CBT. However, the emerging integration of mindfulness-based strategies shows promise, with researchers working toward operationalizing elements of mindfulness that may influence symptom reduction, and the rise of qualitative evidence toward this end. The improvement of skills-based learning within these strategies shows early results in influencing stress and anxiety reduction and coping strategies, with more research needed in this area (Dariotis et al., 2016; Hayes, Villatte, Levin, & Hildebrandt, 2011).

Helping professionals may note that there are differences in presenting issues that fall under the broad category of stress and anxiety. For instance, clients may present with primarily physical concerns (shortness of breath, racing heart, etc.), cognitive concerns (rumination, obsessional thinking, etc.), or emotional concerns (dread, fear, etc.). This is an area that could be explored with more depth, particularly differing treatment approaches for different presentations. This line of research could also influence future directions on the definitions and classifications of anxiety-based diagnoses found in the *Diagnostic and Statistical Manual of Mental Disorders* (American Psychological Association, 2013) and the *International Statistical Classification of Diseases and Related Health Problems* (World Health Organization, 1992).

In addition to exploring elements of stress and anxiety, helping professionals may note differences in the clients seeking support. For instance, research and professional approaches exploring differences with clients who experience future-based worries (ex. what ifs?), and those who experience past-based worries (ex. if only I hadn't) may improve techniques and interventions. Further, differences when working with clients who are experiencing anxiety for the first time and those who have been dealing with chronic or lifelong anxiety deserve a critical lens.

Recent research around stress and anxiety has been focused on neurochemistry and brain-based biology. This focus will likely continue in the future as technology and accessibility continue to improve. Growth in this area continues the development of more effective anti-anxiety medications, with some considering that anxiety concerns may be wholly resolved through biomedical means. Missing from these developments, however, is an understanding of the mechanisms underlying these treatments—that is, we generally know what impact medications are having, but not necessarily how this impact occurs. Interestingly, not only the brain, but other parts of the body, may be implicated in anxiety concerns. Recent research shows that targeting microbes in the digestive system may also play a part in affecting levels of stress (Schmidt, 2015).

Finally, continued exploration of resilience, and protective factors against developing pathological levels of stress and anxiety, deserve mention. Tailored positive psychology interventions are emerging in health care centers, high-risk schools, and neighborhoods as a means to protect community members from the strain of stress and anxiety, and as a preventive measure to reduce the disruptive nature of symptoms. While in its infancy, this direction highlights the use of community-oriented cognitive, physiological, and emotional prevention strategies to support disruptive stress and anxiety responses (Muller et al., 2016; Smokowski et al., 2016; Sokoloski & Necka, 2016). Although stress and anxiety (along with depression) have been studied more than most mental health concerns, as knowledge and practice expands, so too do the demands for research in these areas.

▶ INTERVENTIONS IN THIS CHAPTER

Psychoeducational

Ug the Caveman (page 7): This intervention explains the physiology underlying the fight-or-flight response, normalizing much of the stress reaction.

Talk-Based/Motivational

Holes in the Sand (page 10) : Through the use of a metaphor, this intervention helps the client to develop alternative thoughts or belief patterns.

Art-Based

Draw the Breath (page 13): This intervention offers a visualization of the breath, with the added element of the art and practice of slowing down and expanding the breath.

Hands-On

Blowing Bubbles (page 16): Inspiring playfulness and creativity, this intervention encourages novel ways to consider breathing while in stressful situations.

Relational

Finger Push-ups (page 19): Clients will notice the physiological needs of the body and learn a physical technique to decrease the intensity of the physiological stress experience.

Group

My Friend Anxiety (page 22): This intervention is designed to encourage group participants to notice the finer details of the stress or anxiety reaction, as well as possible strategies that can be used to alleviate unwanted symptoms.

Homework

The Definition of Success (page 27): This intervention encourages clients to expand upon their current definitions and expectations, which may be contributing to increased stress.

▶ UG THE CAVEMAN

AMOUNT OF TIME

25 minutes

MATERIALS NEEDED

- Whiteboard
- Dry-erase marker(s)
- Paper (optional)
- Colored markers/pencils (optional)

Type of Activity

Psychoeducational

Intent/Used for . . .

This activity is designed to introduce the idea that stress and anxiety are naturally occurring reactions in our bodies, and are, in fact, beneficial. The activity also creates an awareness of the physiological underpinnings of stress, which in turn can normalize some of the symptoms clients are experiencing.

Step-by-Step Instructions

1. Introduce the topic by mentioning that you'd like to share a thought experiment about other people who experience stress—cavepeople.
2. Using a whiteboard or blank piece of paper, draw a caveperson (a stick person with a club, or any other similar likeness) and invite the client to name the character—the remainder of the intervention will refer to the caveperson as 'Ug.'
3. Draw a dinosaur off to the side of the caveperson (there is no need for the art to be perfect).
4. Invite the client to brainstorm things that might be going on in Ug's body as soon as Ug sees the dinosaur (see the physiological reactions listed under Guiding Questions).
5. As the client says a symptom, draw it on the caveperson. For example, with the heart beating faster, draw a big heart on the figure—it often helps to inject a sense of humor to the drawing.

Figure 1.1 Clients will often appreciate seeing a clear connection between physiology and stress—regardless of your artistic ability.

6. Most clients will not list all of the relevant symptoms, so often the helping professional will need to provide a few.
7. Once the drawing part is complete, invite the client to consider the purpose of each part of the stress reaction—that is, why would Ug need this to happen, when faced with a threat?
8. With each item, relate the information to symptoms that the client has experienced. Emphasize that these reactions are typical, though not everybody experiences them in the same way, and there are very beneficial reasons for them to occur.
9. Bring the conversation back into the present, highlighting that while in the present-day we do not experience dinosaurs, we still experience the stress reaction.

Guiding Questions

- What types of things are like dinosaurs for *you*?
- Can you think of some things Ug can do in order to help his body with this reaction?
- The physiological reactions we normally address (and why they occur) are:
  - *Heart rate increases (adrenaline and oxygen to the muscles/brain)*
  - *Breathing rate increases (increased oxygen—food for the brain)*
  - *Muscles tighten (preparing to fight/flee from that dinosaur!)*
  - *Thoughts increase/become rapid (thinking about ways to escape/fight)*
  - *Attention/eyes focus (gathering information about dinosaur/threat)*
  - *Sweating increases (cools body down while other parts are increasing heat)*
  - *Immune system suppressed (not crucial right now—body needs system's energy)*
  - *Digestive system suppressed (not crucial right now—body needs system's energy)*

Tips/Ways to Change

- You may need to adapt/shorten the list of items for younger clients. I typically will stick with the brain, muscles, and heart.
- Be sure to establish rapport before jumping into what may be seen as a 'kids' activity'!
- Alternatively, invite the client to imagine a tiger jumping into the office, and reflect on what may go on in their body if that were to happen.
- If materials are scarce, this can be a talk-only activity, though most clients find that watching the helping professional draw—albeit poorly—is a fun activity. The addition of the image will support the client in recalling the information shared.
- If time permits, or if it is relevant, you can also spend some time looking at the detrimental effects each of these symptoms may have if continued for an extended period of time.
- This activity is a nice way to begin introducing stress and anxiety management techniques, as most techniques are associated with at least one physiological response (for example, muscle relaxation targets both attention and muscle tension).

NOTES

▶ HOLES IN THE SAND

AMOUNT OF TIME

15–20 minutes

MATERIALS NEEDED

- Paper (optional)
- Pen/markers (optional)

Type of Activity

Talk-based/Motivational

Intent/Used for . . .

For many clients dealing with stress or anxiety concerns, the initial goals include reducing, or even eliminating, automatic thoughts. Although this is a reasonable goal, the focus is on what needs to 'go away' rather than what the client would like to 'be there' instead. Using the metaphor of trying to dig holes in the sand, this intervention helps a client to develop a number of possible, alternative thoughts or beliefs, which may be able to replace the stressful thoughts.

Note that this intervention is very useful for initial stages of CBT or other cognitive-based therapies, and as such will be more practical in the first or second session of a multi-session framework.

Step-by-Step Instructions

1. Begin by inviting the client to consider somebody wanting to dig permanent holes in a sandbox. Explain that in order for the person to dig a hole in the sand, some of the sand must be removed. However, if simply removing sand is the only strategy, the hole will be filled back in overnight due to the natural tendencies of sand.
2. Invite the client to consider how the sand could be prevented from filling back into the newly formed hole. Take two to three minutes to brainstorm ideas.
3. Emphasizing an idea that may already have been presented by the client, note that one of the best ways to prevent sand falling back into the hole is to place something new, or more solid, in the hole, thus allowing the hole to solidify overnight.
4. Explain to the client that the sandbox is very similar to our minds, with sand taking the place of thoughts. The hole-filling nature of sand is akin to automatic thoughts. With this in mind, while it is important to identify stressful or anxiety-provoking thoughts that the client may not want to think about, it is equally, if not more, important to discover what possible replacement thoughts might look like. Otherwise, there is the very real possibility that the original, automatic thoughts may fill back in, just like in a sandbox.
5. After giving the client some space to consider and respond to this notion, explain that you will together be brainstorming what some of these new thoughts might look like. It is important to emphasize that the new thoughts may not yet be believable, but having them at-the-ready is integral to reducing stressful and anxiety-related thought processes.
6. Invite the client to identify two to three thoughts that are commonly linked to stress or anxiety. Acknowledge the very real emotions that are connected to these thoughts and beliefs.
7. Explain to the client that, using these thoughts as the 'sand,' you will together discover some possibilities for some replacement thoughts, in three different ways.
8. First, invite the client to list at least one thought or belief that would directly oppose an automatic and stressful thought. For example, if the automatic thought is 'I will not get a job,' a possible opposition could be 'I will get a job.' Again, emphasize that not all of these thoughts will immediately be believable, which is fine for the moment.

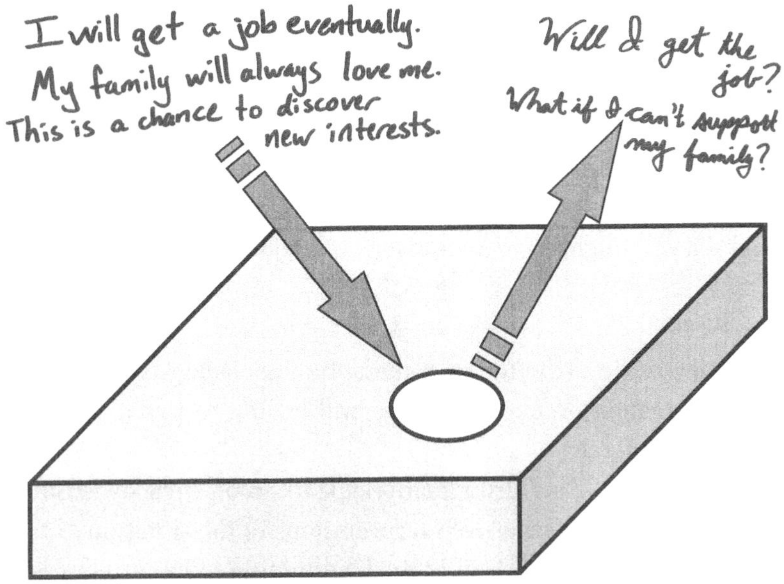

Figure 1.2 It can be just as important to focus on the replacement/desired thoughts than it is to focus on the unwanted thoughts.

9. Second, invite the client to develop two to three thoughts or phrases that others may use in similar situations, or which others in their life have told them they should 'think instead.' For example, perhaps a family member has told them that 'Even if they don't get a job, they will still be supported financially.'
10. Third, invite the client to look at the situation itself that has led to the automatic thoughts being stressful, and develop two to three thoughts that could be alternative interpretations to the situation. For example, if the client does not have a job, one interpretation could be 'I have more time to spend with my children.'
11. Summarize the various alternative thoughts, and invite the client to pick two to three alternatives that seem to reflect the most with them—thoughts or beliefs that feel the most 'solid' and could possibly hold at least some of the sand back.
12. Congratulate the client on getting to this point—discovering some thoughts to aim toward, rather than trying to avoid the undesirable thoughts. This is very difficult to do, but shows great promise for working with automatic thoughts over the coming sessions.

Guiding Questions

- Have you ever played in the sand, either on the beach or in a sandbox? What types of things did you do or make in the sand?
- What are some ways that (in real life) we could prevent the sand from filling back into the hole overnight?
- Right now it may feel like you are trying to remove the sand—your automatic thoughts—to make space for something else. What are some of those automatic thoughts or beliefs that are stressful?

- Even if you don't believe them at all, what are some thoughts that are the exact opposite of those automatic ones?
- What types of things do the people in your life say, or what would they say, when you tell them about some of these stressful thoughts? What are their suggestions?
- What is typically happening when these thoughts come up? What are the common stressful situations and are there other possible interpretations to what is going on?
- Which of these new thoughts or beliefs feels the most 'solid' to you? Which one or two does your gut tell you might have the most power to keep the sand at bay for a little while?

Tips/Ways to Change

- Some clients may respond better to a metaphor, replacing thoughts with some movie scenes involving stealing precious artifacts and having to replace them with something similar but slightly different.
- Younger clients may find the third step difficult to do on their own, and may need some guidance in finding some alternative interpretations to the situation.
- As mentioned, this intervention is only the beginning step in developing a different pathway for automatic thoughts. For possible strategies that can follow this activity, Robert Leahy has written a great book, *Cognitive Therapy Techniques* (2003), with a number of cognitive-based interventions.

NOTES

▶ DRAW THE BREATH

Type of Activity

Art-based

AMOUNT OF TIME

10 minutes

Intent/Used for . . .

This activity is designed to help ground the client to reduce anxiety symptoms through focusing on the breath and small movements. This activity offers a visualization of the breath, with an added element of art, as well as an intentional practice to slow and expand the breath.

MATERIALS NEEDED

- Paper
- Crayons

Step-by-Step Instructions

1. Offer the client a piece of paper and a number of different colors of crayons. Invite the client to choose one color from the options.
2. Invite the client to place the tip of their crayon in the center of the paper. While demonstrating, invite the client to inhale, drawing a spiral out from the center, and exhale, spiraling back into the center. Be flexible, be creative, and allow the client to be creative. Offer encouragement as art directives may be new and cause additional stress for the client.

Figure 1.3 Notice the difference in how the body feels between the small, tighter breath, and the breath that expands farther outward. Try three breaths.

3. Choose a second color. Invite the client to try the spiral breath again, but this time expanding the breath and the spiral beyond the limits of the first. Place the crayon in the center of the paper. While inhaling, spiral out. While exhaling, spiral in.
4. Choose a third color. With this final set of breaths and spirals, invite the client to attempt to pull the breath all the way out to the edges of the paper. Acknowledge that this is challenging, as it is difficult to control the breath and control the movement of the breath through the arm at the same time. Share strategies for a long and steady breath that you might know.
5. Invite the client to reflect on the art of the breath that has been created in-session. Invite the client to notice how they feel differently now that they have been breathing differently. Explore whether this activity was difficult, or easy. Encourage the client to recognize that there are many ways to use breathing as a grounding technique; this is simply one way to focus on the breath.
6. Remind the client to remember, and possibly even recreate, this experience at home. Acknowledge that a full breath can be both important and beautiful.

Guiding Questions

- Is there any relevance to the color(s) that you chose? Do any of them connect with thinking about or experiencing the breath?
- Have you ever tried controlling your breath before? Why is it difficult? When is it easy?
- Is this the same as your other attempts at controlling your breath? Why or why not?
- How are the three breaths different on the page? Did you notice any difference when you were breathing these breaths?
- This activity is usually difficult to start but gets easier with each try. Did you find that to be true for you?
- Do you feel any different (physically or emotionally) now, compared to at the start of the session? How does this connect with strategies to reduce some of the stress and anxiety concerns that we have been discussing?
- What do you think you will remember about this activity?

Tips/Ways to Change

- I typically complete this intervention along with the client, so that the client can look toward my modeling of the breathing, and spiraling, and pace along with me if necessary. This may also reduce some anxiety experienced by the client in creating an art image.
- With young clients, or with clients who have challenges with complex instructions, you can invite the client to simply draw a circle over and over, rather than a spiral. While this does not always offer the same visualizations of an expanded breath as a spiral, it still offers the option to see the breath.
- I intentionally offer crayons for this activity (over colored pencils or markers) because crayons offer the additional benefit of allowing pressure changes within the movement of this activity.
- I often model for the client that the trick to a good inhale is starting with a complete exhale, and I demonstrate by exhaling deeply so the lungs are completely empty.
- If time allows, invite the client to color in the spiral however they like during discussion and reflection afterwards.

NOTES

BLOWING BUBBLES

AMOUNT OF TIME

5 minutes

MATERIALS NEEDED

- Bubble solution
- Bubble wand

Type of Activity

Hands-on

Intent/Used for . . .

This activity offers a non-dialogic method of exploring the use of the breath to reduce anxiety and stress symptoms. An added benefit of this activity is that it often inspires playfulness and noticing beauty, which can generate positive emotions and further conversation on how these types of activities alleviate distressing symptoms.

Step-by-Step Instructions

1. Introduce the discussion of controlling and monitoring the breath as a method of stress or anxiety management. Most clients will have heard or considered at some point that taking a deep breath helps to reduce symptoms of intense arousal. However, this often proves challenging in the moment, and sometimes clients feel self-conscious when practicing breathing activities in the session.
2. Invite the client to recall the last time they experienced blowing bubbles. Listen and reflect on the client's experience, reflecting any emotions that you might perceive.
3. Invite the client to try blowing bubbles, at first just to practice. Allow the client to have some fun with blowing bubbles for a few minutes, before continuing with the directed bubble blowing.

Figure 1.4 Bubble blowing offers a playful visualization of the breath.

4. Discuss the use of bubble blowing to practice controlling the breath. Bubble blowing allows us to *see* the success of our breathing control as the bubble provides evidence of overcoming the difficulties of controlling the breath.
5. Challenge the client to blow anxiety-breath bubbles. This will likely result in either many small bubbles or a dripping mess. Explore the outcomes with the client and, if relevant, the challenges of these types of breaths and whether they feel satisfactory.
6. Challenge the client to try to blow the biggest bubble possible. Share with the client that a deep and satisfying breath depends on a deep exhale that flattens the lungs, followed by a slow and full inhale and a gentle and controlled exhale. Model this for the client, if necessary, then invite the client to use this controlled exhale to create the biggest bubble possible.
7. Invite the client to try again.
8. Invite the client to notice what it was like to control the breath, and watch the bubbles grow. Discuss how the client feels in this moment. If appropriate, further discuss the playfulness of bubble blowing and how this has influenced the client's present feelings.
9. Reflect on this playful way to explore controlling breathing, continuing if necessary with a few other anxiety or stress breaths, such as those emerging when sighing or crying, and the breathing that is released when yawning or laughing. Discuss the benefits of a full breath. If appropriate, explore the client's experience of playfulness with blowing bubbles in-session and how this may influence the client's present feelings.

Guiding Questions

- When is the last time you played with bubbles?
- What is the difference between the long, slow breath bubble and the small, sharp breath bubble?
- What do you notice about yourself and your breathing from doing this activity?
- Why do you think this activity is important or unimportant? What is therapeutic about this activity, if anything?
- How is blowing bubbles similar to what you might know about meditation or other controlled-breathing activities?
- What gets in the way of being playful? How is being playful helpful for mental health?
- Is this what you expected to be doing today in therapy?
- How does this connect to some of the conversations that we have been having about anxiety and stress relief? What are you most likely to remember from today?

Tips/Ways to Change

- Note that bubbles are simply soap. Bubbles on the office carpet, furniture, or clothing—unless silk or leather—are unlikely to do any damage.
- In some households, blowing bubbles while inside is (or was) against the rules. If this arises in discussion, reflect on how this may have influenced the client's experience in-session.
- Allow the client to take the bubbles home, if possible. The price paid for a small bottle of bubbles is typically low in relation to the effectiveness of this intervention. Invite the client to blow bubbles at least once as homework.

NOTES

FINGER PUSH-UPS

Type of Activity

Relational

AMOUNT OF TIME

5 minutes

MATERIALS NEEDED

- None

Intent/Used for . . .

This intervention invites the client to pay attention to the physiological needs of the body. Through a localized and easy hand exercise, the client and helping professional can discuss and model a tense/release practice. This results in decreasing the intensity of the physiological response to stress and anxiety in-session, and adds to the client's repertoire of accessible management tools.

Step-by-Step Instructions

1. Briefly introduce the client to the physiological response related to stress and anxiety (see Ug the Cavemen, page 7), emphasizing the body's desire to move, whether it be to fight, flee, freeze, or collapse. Validate the practical difficulties in running, fighting, freezing, or collapsing in everyday life, offering this activity toward addressing immediate needs for body movement when stress or anxiety feel physiologically intense.
2. Demonstrate the pose to the client, placing your hands together in front of your chest, palms together, in a prayer-type posture.
3. Invite the client to mimic this pose, without adding any pressure to the hands.
4. Invite the client to notice in what parts of their body they feel muscle tension or activation, even without adding any pressure to the palms. Share with the client where you might feel tension or activation of muscles, paying particular attention to areas where the client might not immediately notice activation, such as across the back or chest, the neck, and the belly or core.
5. Invite the client to gently press their hands together and hold this posture for a moment, naming a different area that now feels muscle tension or activation. Support and validate the client's responses and participation, perhaps naming additional muscles that are activated, such as facial muscles, if the client is smiling or frowning.
6. Invite the client to relax, placing the hands in a resting position. Encourage the client to name the parts of the body that now feel the sensation of release, noticing the difference between tension and release.
7. Invite the client to try the same posture, again pressing the palms gently together to hold the posture. With fingers loose, press the tips of the fingers together to slightly bend the knuckles, but keep the palms pressed together. Count five repetitions, slowly.
8. Encourage the client to now try engaging the fingers in a push-up, using the tips of the fingers to bring the palms away from each other, resulting in the palms moving away from each other and the arms shifting slightly. Count five repetitions, slowly.
9. Invite the client to relax, placing the hands in a resting position. Again, encourage the client to name the parts of the body that now feel relief or release from the tension, noticing the difference between tension and relaxation.

Figure 1.5 Palms together, press fingers together, then add more pressure to lift the palms apart. Release, and notice the difference between 'tense' and 'relax.'

10. Engage the client in describing what tension and relaxation feel like. Invite the client to notice if any of the tensing activities feel similar to their experiences of anxiety or stress. Discuss what it feels like to intensely notice small acts of relief, such as when relaxing the hands. Explore the client's experience into intentionally noticing what muscle release feels like, with the same intensity of attention that one would notice tension and activation. Reflect on how this might influence mood, or an anxiety or stress response.
11. Explore the relevance of body tension in relation to anxiety and stress. Invite the client to try this tension/relaxation activity, with intentional noticing, as a preventive practice in relation to stress or anxiety.

Guiding Questions

- Why do tense/release activities help with a reduction of stress and anxiety?
- What are some of your favorite tension postures? Where do you notice that you tense up naturally or intuitively, or places where you feel tight?
- What works for you presently to notice and release that tension?
- Why do we need tension?
- How does actively focusing on tension in the hands help to relieve some of your natural tension in other areas of the body?
- Do you know anyone else who uses tense/release activities to manage stress? Have you heard of this before?
- How would this be easy for you? How would this be difficult for you?
- How does this fit with some of the things we have been discussing about stress and anxiety concerns?

Tips/Ways to Change

- It is very important to note that manual dexterity and the absence of musculoskeletal pain is required in this activity. The client should be free from pain or injury, especially in the upper body, arms, wrists, and hands.
- Alternate movements, including pressing the soles of the feet into the ground. Finger push-ups against the arms of a chair or against a tabletop, as opposed to pressing the hands together, also offers a similar physiological experience. Additionally, standing push-ups against a wall are useful for activating tense/release.
- If you find the client is struggling with naming or identifying parts of the body, encourage them by naming what you notice as the counselor, both what you feel in your own body and what you see in the client's body.
- Be specific in naming where the release of the muscles is felt in the hands and arms after this period of tension. Invite the client to describe this sensation deeply, using words like 'softening,' 'tingling,' or 'flowing.'
- Invite the client to describe other physical activities they engage in intuitively, such as stretching, yawning, uncrossing the legs, or other tense/release activities you have observed in-session. Use excitement and validation to confirm the client's intuitive knowledge toward the needs of the body, and the relief experienced from dynamic tension and release.

NOTES

MY FRIEND ANXIETY

AMOUNT OF TIME

20–30 minutes

MATERIALS NEEDED

- Paper
- Markers or crayons
- Prompts (see instructions)
- Table
- Colored paper (optional)
- Grommets (optional)

Type of Activity

Group

Intent/Used for . . .

This intervention encourages a creative approach for chunking the stress and anxiety response into small, manageable pieces. Further, this activity encourages discussion of the needs of stress and anxiety, and how these needs might be present in the body. The group activity consolidates the smaller factors of stress and anxiety, with suggested reflection toward identifying small physiological triggers and strategies for reducing these triggers. The participants may also be invited to brainstorm alternate behavioral choices when responding to these triggers.

Step-by-Step Instructions

1. Invite a group discussion on the influence that stress and anxiety have on thoughts, feelings, and the body. Consider integrating education on the physiological underpinnings of the stress response, such as those offered in the Ug the Caveman (page 7) or Rainbow of Experience (page 46) interventions.
2. Give each participant a piece of paper and something to write with. Markers are the preference for this activity; however, crayons, pastels, or colored pencils will also do.
3. Give each participant an individual prompt including these words: Head; Neck & Shoulders; Chest; Belly; Arms & Hands; Legs & Feet. You can randomly assign these prompts, or invite the participants to choose if desired. If you have a greater number of participants, they can be paired, or two separate collective bodies can be created.
4. Invite the participants to consider the needs of stress and anxiety, and how those needs are often enacted differently on different parts of the body. For example, stress may result in the desire to clench and unclench a fist. This is an indicator that stress or anxiety is desiring or preparing for some kind of action in the body.
5. Instruct the participants to use one chosen color to draw or write on their sheets of paper what stress or anxiety desires from their prompted section of the body. Encourage creativity and personalization of answers, suggesting to individual participants that their responses do not necessarily have to be true for everyone, but can be true individually. Limit this portion of the activity to a maximum of five minutes.
6. As this is a group experience, if individuals are showing difficulty, and it is appropriate for the group, invite the participants to request and provide assistance from each other, as needed.
7. Give participants a one-minute warning, and encourage them to think of three more things that might be signals of a stress or anxiety response in this part of the body. If participants appear challenged, offer some sensory indicators, such as tingling or hair-raising, that may present new ideas for a client.
8. Invite the participants to choose a second color to draw or write with. Invite the participants to use this second color to draw or write one specific thing that may result in

Figure 1.6 Invite group members to use two different colors: one for the anxiety response in this part of the body, the other for an approach to reduce anxiety in this part of the body.

a reduction of stress or anxiety in this part of the body. Encourage the participants to consider actions that can be done individually and privately. For example, the desire to clench and unclench a fist might be reduced by stretching the hands and fingers. Encourage creativity, and invite the participants to consider activities for parts of the body that they may not have considered before. If the participants are struggling, again invite assistance from each other, if appropriate.

9. Bring the participants' attention back to the large group. Using space on the floor or on a long table, invite the group members to piece together My Friend Anxiety, the body created from the collective parts. This portion of the activity can be completed with as much creativity as desired; piecing together square paper offers a semi-robotic look.
10. Encourage exploration and discussion of My Friend Anxiety. Invite the participants to share which of these physiological responses they may feel are familiar, and which are new. Offer time for discussion and reflection on the experience of creation in a group.
11. Reflect on the often-overwhelming physical sensation of stress and anxiety, in conjunction with the power of a small and specific physiological intervention. Invite the group members to share any additional strategies that they may use to reduce arousal when needed, and add these items to My Friend Anxiety as appropriate.

12. If time allows, invite the participants to choose one of the strategies offered, and to try it in the group, with discussion on practicing approaches to reducing stress and anxiety in the body.
13. If appropriate, offer a handout based on the information below (see the Guiding Questions section), inviting the participants to add any additional activities that they find helpful.

Guiding Questions

- What was easy/difficult about this activity?
- Did you work on the part of the body that you normally feel in response to stress?
- What part(s) did someone else work on that you can relate to? Are your strategies similar? Different?
- For the strategies that you chose—is this something that you have tried before?
- My Friend Anxiety, when put together, may seem pretty intense. What is it like to see this, given your experience of stress or anxiety?
- Most of the time when we experience stress or anxiety, we do not notice all of these parts all of the time. What would you do to help a person like My Friend Anxiety? Are there things you would say to My Friend Anxiety? How would you act around this Friend that would be helpful?
- What strategy do you see here that you did not consider before?
- Which strategy would you like to try?
- What is one thing you will remember from today that you think will be helpful for your own concerns?

Adapt the following as a handout for the group:

Softening the Body

HEAD

- Relax the jaw muscles and tongue.
- Smile.
- Cover your ears with your cupped hands and listen to 'the ocean.'
- ______________________________
- ______________________________

NECK & SHOULDERS

- Place your hand on the back of your neck and notice the temperature difference between your hand and your neck.
- Soften the shoulders and, simultaneously, raise your head and neck straight up, pulling the neck long.
- Using both hands, use your fingertips to gently tap and rub along the middle of your neck, giving yourself a gentle massage. Include your shoulders, if desired.
- ______________________________
- ______________________________

ARMS & HANDS

- Open your fingers wide. Using your opposite hand, gently pull back on your fingers, toward your forearm, for a stretch around your wrist and inner arm.
- Link your fingers together and pull, for a powerful stretch through your arms and back.
- Gently pinch around the edges of your palm for a light hand massage.
- ______________________________
- ______________________________

CHEST

- Counting down from three, take three full breaths.
- Place your hand flat on your chest. Notice the temperature difference between your hand and your chest.
- Sit up straight and pull your shoulders back, opening up the space across your chest. If you have the space, open up your arms and pull your shoulders back, saying "Ah" aloud.
- ______________________________
- ______________________________

BELLY

- Place one or both hands on your belly and feel the rise and fall of your belly for three breaths.
- Use small, gentle circles to rub your belly for 10 seconds.
- Exhale fully, until the lungs are flat. Inhale fully, and focus on the expansion of the belly, trying to fill the belly with breath as much as possible.
- ______________________________
- ______________________________

LEGS & FEET

- While sitting, bring your feet up to your toes slowly, tightening your calves. Slowly lower. Repeat two more times.
- While sitting, draw your toes up in the air, tightening your shins. Slowly lower. Repeat two more times.
- Press the heels of your feet into the floor. Open the toes wide and roll the soles of the feet flat to the floor all the way through the toes, trying to touch the floor with as much of the sole of the foot as possible.
- ______________________________
- ______________________________

Tips/Ways to Change

- There are a number of ways this activity can be altered, depending on the goals of the group. Rather than exploring large sections of the body, participants can be invited to explore smaller sections of the head, with the prompts of: Eyes, Nose, Mouth, Ears, Jaw.

- With groups greater than six, this activity can be further separated to include a number of body parts/areas.
- This activity can become a carousel-type activity, adding movement around the room. Situate the different body sections with labeled prompts around the room. Allow each participant to respond to the activity for one minute, then rotate to the next section. Repeat this movement with strategies for reducing arousal.
- This activity can be used to explore the state opposing a stress or anxiety response, such as My Friend Settled or My Friend Mindful. Invite participants to explore how these characteristics feel in the different parts of the body, and what these states want the body to do.

NOTES

▶ THE DEFINITION OF SUCCESS

Type of Activity

Homework

AMOUNT OF TIME

Explanation: 20 minutes

Debrief: 15 minutes

MATERIALS NEEDED

- Paper (optional)
- Pen (optional)
- Dictionary (optional)

Intent/Used for . . .

This homework can be used in many instances, and it is particularly useful when the client seems to be having difficulty with external pressures or stressors arising from relationships with others. Challenging ideas about success also can be poignant for clients who are working through issues with perfectionism. It is suitable to assign this homework in the first or second session to get the client invested in change. The activity of producing an ideal definition can be empowering, and will often lead to reflection about the client's sources of stress.

Step-by-Step Instructions

1. Explain to the client that sometimes our definitions of certain words can influence how we see the world, and, by extension, ourselves.
2. Invite the client to consider what the definition of the word 'success' is for other people in the client's life (family, friends, employer, partner, etc.). If they are comfortable in doing so, invite the client to share with you what some of those definitions are.
3. Invite the client to consider what their own definition of the word 'success' is. After giving some space for this reflection, invite them to share this definition with you.
4. Explain to the client that for their homework, you will be inviting them to do some more reflection about the definition(s) of the word 'success.'

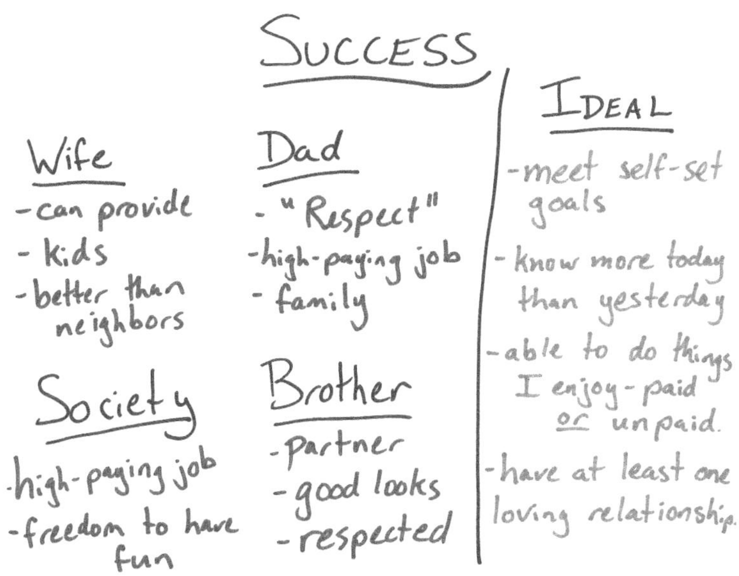

Figure 1.7 Recognizing and taking ownership over our own internalized definitions can be a powerful activity.

5. For their homework, invite the client to consider the current definition of 'success' for the people around them, but even more generally, for the greater population and society as a whole—what definition of 'success' do people subscribe to?
6. After reflecting on this, as a second part to the homework, invite the client to consider and develop their own, ideal definition of 'success'—not simply a definition that they themselves would like to have in their lives, but a definition of 'success' by which everybody in society could (or should) live.
7. Encourage the client to write down their new/ideal definition and bring it to the following session.

Debrief

1. Invite the client to share their ideal definition of success.
2. Invite the client to consider the process behind the homework, and how easy or difficult it was for them to complete.
3. Encourage the client to highlight any differences, and similarities, between the current definition(s) and their ideal definition.
4. Invite the client to consider how their relationships, decisions, and day-to-day living would be different if their ideal definition of success was the current definition.
5. Check in with the client about their stress or anxiety—how has it changed through completing this homework? How does their own definition of success (or other words) contribute to how they experience stress?

Guiding Questions

- Before I begin explaining this homework, what do you think are some of the common themes in the thoughts that give you the most stress?
- How do you think (your boss, your partner, etc.) defines success?
- How do you currently define success? Is there some sort of checklist that is inherent in the definition? What needs to be met in order to say that something or someone is a success?
- What has changed about your own definition since you were younger?
- If you have the chance to rewrite the 'societal dictionary,' the definitions that everybody in general subscribes to, how would you *want* success to be defined? How would the checklist for success be different?

Debrief

- How was this homework for you? Did an ideal definition come easily?
- What is your ideal definition? How does that differ from your current definition? From others'?
- If your ideal definition was the actual/current definition, how would this change what is currently going on in your life?
- What could you take away from this activity? How does your definition of success contribute to the stress or anxiety that you've been feeling?

Tips/Ways to Change

- This homework as a whole can easily be divided into multiple parts—the initial homework can be to discover and then record others' definitions of 'success,' followed by the client's current definition, and finally looking at what an ideal definition would be.
- One of the biggest changes that can easily be made to this homework is to change the word that is to be defined—'success' works for many clients; however, other suggestions could be 'power,' 'happiness,' 'perfect,' or even 'healthy relationship.'
- With younger children, this activity could be adapted to be an in-session intervention, encouraging the client to create a small dictionary of definitions. Depending on the client's age and reading level, use of an already-existing dictionary may be useful to get things started.
- Sometimes, a client's definition of 'success' is not unique from the other people in their life. If this is the case, it is important to explore why this may be before continuing with the intervention.
- If a client is having difficulty with the notion of changing definitions, be sure to emphasize that this is merely a 'thought experiment' and that they are not rewriting or necessarily even changing their current definitions. Note that they may be surprised at how much this simple experiment can change their views, and by extension, their levels of stress or anxiety.
- Be sure to debrief with the client when they return, regardless of if they have completed the homework or not.

NOTES

▶ OTHER RESOURCES

Abel, J. (2014). *Resistant anxiety, worry, and panic: 86 practical treatment strategies for clinicians.* Eau Claire, WI: PESI Publishing & Media.

Arden, J. B. (2014). *Brain based therapy for anxiety: Workbook for clinicians & clients.* Eau Claire, WI: PESI Publishing & Media.

Bourne, E. J. (2011). *The anxiety and phobia workbook* (5th ed.). Oakland, CA: New Harbinger Publications.

Chen, D. D. & Kottler, J. A. (2012). *Stress management and prevention: Applications to daily life* (2nd ed.). New York, NY: Routledge.

Emmett, R. (2008). *Manage your time to reduce your stress: A handbook for the overworked, overscheduled, and overwhelmed.* New York, NY: Walker Publishing Company.

Leahy, R. L. (2003). *Cognitive therapy techniques: A practitioner's guide.* New York, NY: Guilford.

Quinn, R., Wehner, P., & One Long House. (2015). *Stop, breathe, & think [Software].* Retrieved from http://stopbreathethink.org/.

Salzman, A. (2014). *A still quiet place.* Oakland, CA: New Harbinger Publications.

Sapolsky, R. M. (2004). *Why zebras don't get ulcers* (3rd ed.). New York, NY: Holt Paperback.

Williams, C. (2013). *Overcoming anxiety, stress and panic: A five areas approach* (3rd ed.). London, UK: Hodder Education.

▶ REFERENCES

American Psychiatric Association. (2013). *Diagnostic and statistical manual of mental disorders* (5th ed.). Washington, DC: Author.

American Psychological Association. (2013). College students' mental health is a growing concern, survey finds. *Upfront, 44*(6), 13. Retrieved January 16th, 2016 from http://www.apa.org/monitor/2013/06/college-students.aspx

Baer, R. A. (Ed.). (2006). *Mindfulness-based treatment approaches: Clinician's guide to evidence base and applications.* Burlington, MA: Elsevier.

Bourne, E. J. (2010). *The anxiety and phobia workbook* (5th ed.). Oakland, CA: New Harbinger Publications.

Bracha, H. S., Ralston, T. C., Matsukawa, J. M., Williams, A. E., & Bracha, A. S. (2004). Does "fight or flight" need updating? *Psychosomatics, 45*(5), 448–449. http://dx.doi.org/10.1176/appi.psy.45.5.448 Retrieved January 16th, 2016.

Crocq, M.-A. (2003). Alcohol, nicotine, caffeine, and mental disorders. *Dialogues in Clinical Neuroscience, 5*(2), 175–185. Retrieved January 16th, 2016.

Dariotis, J., Mirabal-Beltran, R., Cluxton-Keller, F., Gould, L. F., Greenberg, M., & Mendelson, T. (2016). A qualitative evaluation of student learning and skills use in a school-based mindfulness and yoga program. *Mindfulness, 7*(1), 76–89. http://doi.org/10.1007/s12671-015-0463-y. Retrieved March 13th, 2016.

Furnham, A. & Lousley, C. (2013). Mental health literacy and the anxiety disorders. *Health, 5*(3A), 521–531. http://dx.doi.org/10.4236/health.2013.53A071 Retrieved January 16th, 2016.

Guindon, M. H. (2011). *A counseling primer: An introduction to the process.* New York, NY: Routledge.

Hayes, S., Villatte, M., Levin, M., & Hildebrandt, M. (2011). Open, aware, and active: Contextual approaches as an emerging trend in the behavioral and cognitive therapies. *Annual Review of Clinical Psychology, 7,* 141–168. http://doi.org/10.1146/annurev-clinpsy-032210-104449 Retrieved March 9th, 2016.

Kimmel, R. J., Roy-Byrne, P. P., & Cowley, D. S. (2015). Pharmacological treatments for panic disorder, generalized anxiety disorder, specific phobia, and social anxiety disorder. In P. E. Nathan & J. M. Gorman (Eds.), *A guide to treatments that work,* 4th ed. (463–506). New York, NY: Oxford University Press.

Leahy, R. L. (2003). *Cognitive therapy techniques: A practitioner's guide.* New York, NY: Guilford.

McEwan, B. S. (2005). Stressed or stressed out: What is the difference? *Journal of Psychiatry and Neuroscience, 30*(5), 315–318. Retrieved January 16th, 2016 from http://www.ncbi.nlm.nih.gov/pmc/articles/PMC1197275/

McGonigal, K. (2015). *The upside of stress: Why stress is good for you, and how to get good at it.* New York, NY: Penguin Random House.

Muller, R., Gertz, K., Molton, I., Terrill, A., Bombardier, C., Ehde, D., & Jensen, M. (2016). Effects of a tailored positive psychology intervention on well-being and pain in individuals with chronic pain and a physical disability: A feasibility trial. *Clinical Journal of Pain, 32*(1), 32–44. http://dx.doi.org/10.1097/AJP.0000000000225 Retrieved March 9th, 2016.

Schmidt, C. (2015). Mental health: Thinking from the gut. *Nature, 518,* S12–S15. http://dx.doi.org/10.1038/518S13a Retrieved January 16th, 2016.

Smokowski, P. R., Guo, S., Evans, C. B., Wu, Q., Rose, R. A., Bacallao, M., & Cotter, K. L. (2016). Risk and protective factors across multiple microsystems associated with internalizing symptoms and aggressive behavior in rural adolescents. *American Journal of Orthopsychiatry.* Abstract retrieved March 9th, 2016 from Europe PMC database: http://europepmc.org/abstract/med/26881984

Sokoloski, H. M. & Necka, E. A. (2016). Remediating math anxiety through cognitive training: Potential roles for math ability and social context. *Journal of Neuroscience, 36*(5), 1439–1441. http://dx.doi.org/10.1523/JNEUROSCI.4039-15.2016 Retrieved March 18th, 2016.

World Health Organization. (1992). *International statistical classification of diseases and related health problems* (10th ed.). Geneva: Author.

2 Low Mood and Depression

▶ WHAT ARE *LOW MOOD AND DEPRESSION* CONCERNS?

In this chapter, we present interventions that may be useful when working with clients who are experiencing lower mood. Although many associate low mood solely with emotions related to sadness, it is essential to note that low mood (and depression) can present in different ways, many of which can influence general motivation and energy levels (American Psychiatric Association, 2013). For the purposes of this chapter, we associate low mood not only with sadness, but also with numbness or the absence of emotion, known as anhedonia. Depression can be experienced by clients in any age group; it is not limited to adults, though there is some evidence that the symptoms are more prevalent in early adulthood (Goldberg, Breckenridge, & Sheikh, 2003). With this in mind, note that even without a diagnosis of a mood disorder, clients at all ages may benefit from the interventions found in this chapter. Below are some examples of what you may hear clients say when presenting with low mood or depression concerns.

"I'm depressed."

As with anxiety, many people are familiar with the term *depression*, so much so that there are concerns that its overuse may be preventing people with a clinical diagnosis of *Major Depressive Disorder* from seeking appropriate supports (Eisenberg, Downs, Golberstein, & Ziven, 2009; Jorm, 2000). Therefore, clients may present with fairly straightforward requests for helping professionals to treat their depressed state. Some education regarding the *Diagnostic and Statistical Manual of Mental Disorders* diagnosis of Major Depressive Disorder (American Psychiatric Association, 2013) can be useful to help the client contextualize what they are experiencing, and helping professionals are recommended to consult a medical or clinical professional should there be concerns about pathology. Typically, it is the symptomology of *low mood* that the client is recognizing, regardless of the terminology they are using.

"I spent the whole day in bed yesterday."

One of the more common concerns that fall under low mood issues is that of *low energy*, or a general sense of tiredness. While it is recommended to track such concerns and establish that this symptom has been occurring for more than just one day, the inability to find energy to leave one's bed can still be considered a significant concern. Overall fatigue can impact the client in a variety of settings, ranging from the workplace to romantic relationships. In these cases, it is worth exploring with the client how they have been able to attend the appointment itself, which in turn may spark a sense of hope in addressing this concern.

"I know I should finish this project, but I just don't feel like it."

A *lack of motivation* is typically seen in clients for whom low mood is a concern, and is especially prevalent in older adults (Fiske, Wetherell, & Gatz, 2009). Different from an outright loss of interest (described below), having little or no motivation means that the client is having difficulty accomplishing task-oriented goals, often despite significant external or internal incentives to do so. An example of this type of lack of motivation would be a client who has a project to finish at work, and who cannot find the drive or desire to complete the final few steps, despite an approaching deadline and threats of salary cuts. While in this scenario there may be additional concerns, such as career or identity (see the Identity chapter on page 157), the client in this example illustrates lack of motivation to the extent that it is disruptive, and it therefore may be indicative of low mood concerns.

"I haven't really wanted to have sex (with anybody) for a while now."

Another common indicator of low mood concerns is a *loss of interest* in previously enjoyable activities. For the above client (not wanting to have sex), this is considered a low mood concern if the client had previously found sex to be enjoyable—it is important for the helping professional to establish that this has indeed been the case, and to not make assumptions about the client's history. As with all of the concerns associated with low mood, there should be a pattern of significant change from the client's usual experience, as one specific instance of not wanting to do an activity is typically not a low mood concern. Other examples of loss of interest include not wanting to engage in hobbies and disconnecting from friendships.

"I'm sick of not getting any better."

Some clients, regardless of their immediate concerns, can present with a feeling of *being stuck*. This feeling can be directly related to low mood—for example, the client has been diagnosed with Major Depressive Disorder, and has tried a number of treatment options with minimal success, or presents with other concerns, such as long-term physical illness or pain.

Regardless, for our purposes, the feeling of being stuck may be an indicator of low mood. This feeling is concerning because it often indicates a *lack of hope*, a serious issue that should be addressed when it arises in session (Allen, 2006). Some of the interventions found in this chapter focus indirectly on re-establishing hope; note that this does not necessarily mean that the client must be seeing everything in a positive light, but rather that the client is able to see that change is possible.

"I just don't see the point."

Another indicator of a lack of hope, a loss of purpose can be devastating to our clients. Sometimes, this 'jaded viewpoint' can be tied directly to a phenomenon known as *burnout*. Burnout is a natural—albeit serious—occurrence, with many people having this experience at least once in their lifetime (Ahola et al., 2006). Essentially, we define burnout as a sense of mental exhaustion directly related to investing too much energy into one particular domain (work, relationships, etc.). Closely associated with burnout, the client may alternatively be experiencing *compassion fatigue*, which shows similar symptomology as a result of caring for others past one's own limits. Much of the management and strategies around burnout is preventative; however, stepping back from the 'energy investment' and emphasizing self-care is also an important part of support for this particular concern.

****A lack of hope, loss of purpose, and feeling stuck are all indicators that a client may be experiencing suicidal ideation. This book does not cover suicide intervention, but please note that a helping professional should never hesitate to ask the question, "Are you thinking about killing yourself?" For more information about suicide and suicide intervention, please refer to the additional resources at the end of this chapter.*** **

▶ RELEVANCE

Along with stress and anxiety, low mood and depression concerns are among the most prevalent counseling issues that arise in our offices. Some studies put low mood concerns at as high as 36% for certain populations (American Psychological Association, 2013). This is concerning, as when left unmanaged or unsupported, low mood—in particular when it is associated with Major Depressive Disorder—has the potential to lead to suicidal ideation, or the formation of suicide planning. Outside of harm to one's physical self, extended periods of acute low mood can also have adverse effects on social relationships and long-term psychological well-being. People who are feeling low have a tendency to distance themselves from social support circles and networks, which in turn can lead to exacerbated poor mental health issues.

It is important to note that humans are emotional beings, and therefore part of the human experience is to occasionally feel sad, lonely, or unmotivated. As with all mental health treatment, the goals for working with clients who have low mood concerns should be regulation and management, rather than elimination of emotion. In fact, even for longer-term depression, recent research has shown that depression itself may serve an adaptive function, though this is still debated (Durisko, Mulsant, & Andrews, 2015). Regardless, clients will continue to approach helping professionals with low mood and depression concerns; although the emotions themselves may be natural, the experience as a whole can be quite discomforting.

▶ WHAT WORKS WELL

Although this book and the contained interventions are grounded in the psychological realm, low mood and depression concerns are often intertwined with biological and physiological underpinnings. There has been much research into medication-based treatment, with antidepressants being among the most prescribed medications in North America, and the numbers continue to rise (Pratt, Brody, & Gu, 2011). Many studies show the effectiveness of medication, in particular when combined with appropriate psychotherapy (Aaronson, Katzman, & Moster, 2015). However, there are also studies showing that medication alone can fall short of successfully treating low mood or depression, and for this reason many helping professionals are hesitant to recommend medication. It is important that helping professionals recognize the influence that the physical body can have on the psychological mind. A general awareness of nutrition, lifestyle, and other physiological connections to mental health is therefore recommended.

Closely related to nutrition, generally healthy lifestyles have shown great merit in both the prevention of and recovery from low mood issues. The tenet of *self-care*, which can include anything from socializing with friends to taking a short walk, is showing promise as a practice that can bolster mood. In particular, physical activity, a long-time recommendation of physicians, is correlated with more positive mental health and increased motivation (Ratey & Hagerman, 2008).

Cognitive Behavioral Therapy (CBT) is one of the most-researched therapeutic frameworks, and was originally developed to specifically help support clients with low mood and depression concerns (Craighead, Johnson, Carey, & Dunlop, 2015). Focusing on cognitions and their interactions with behaviors, CBT is taught at most university- and college-level counseling and therapy programs, and likely needs little introduction here. One of the benefits of the CBT framework is that it can cross multiple modalities, with homework and online/self-help exercises being a cost-effective supplement to in-person treatment. Although not every helping professional agrees with practicing CBT-exclusive therapy, many CBT-based interventions can still be effective when combined with other theoretical frameworks.

Another therapeutic framework that shows promise for working with low mood and depression is Interpersonal Therapy (IPT). Similar to CBT in structure (IPT also includes a homework component), IPT focuses on the relational aspects of a client's life, helping the client to cope with social stressors in a healthy manner (Craighead et al., 2015). Often seen by clients as less 'jargon-filled' than other therapies, IPT can be quite skill-based and therefore accessible to clients who are looking for practical takeaways.

▶ FUTURE RESEARCH

Similar to stress and anxiety, much of the emerging research around low mood and depression is focusing on advancements with brain imagery, and exploring how the brain and neurochemistry interact in a depressive state. As antidepressants are so frequently prescribed, there continues to be hope that the mechanism by which these medications work may be explored, and by extension will grant insight into possible prevention or minimizing incidents of low mood symptoms. When considering the initial stages of symptoms, there is currently a lack of research around the early warning signs for low mood or depression; it is possible these signs may be biological, physiological, behavioral, or cognitive. It is also important to recognize that depression may actually be an evolved adaptation (Durisko et al., 2015); further research in this area is crucial to framing many of the underlying biological and physiological aspects of these concerns.

Definitions and classifications of mood-related disorders are constantly being updated and revised (American Psychiatric Association, 2013; World Health Organization, 1992), which speaks to many of the differences in how clients may present. For example, helping professionals may note that some clients will present with primarily low motivation and related symptoms, whereas others will present with intense sadness and emotional-based symptoms. Though these are both currently considered signs of low mood, future research may discover that effective treatment for these clients may actually be quite different. Many clients also experience a significant reoccurrence of low mood or depressive episodes, often despite the use of the most up-to-date therapeutic interventions and strategies. It will be important to look into how to minimize this phenomenon, which could lead to changes in what is considered effective treatment.

Within the therapeutic setting, as noted above, many helping professionals support the use of CBT-based frameworks and interventions. In order to be successful, these strategies often rely on the client completing homework between sessions, which has been a source of frustration for many helping professionals, given that the completion rate of homework is typically quite low. Future research looking into how to best encourage clients and ensure the completion of homework would greatly benefit the field as a whole.

A more recent development in the therapeutic field has been focused on clients' time perspective—that is, whether their thoughts tend to focus on past, present, or future, and how they view these periods (positively or negatively). A fair amount of research has already been completed, looking at how the time perspective of a client can significantly impact their healing and therapeutic success (Stolarski, Fleulaine, & van Beek, 2015). However, there still is much to be done to translate this research into concrete strategies and interventions. As with most domains of human psychology, every advance forward in the treatment of low mood and depression seems to create both excitement and further questions—new research and perspectives are always welcomed, as the field will continue to grow in the foreseeable future.

▶ INTERVENTIONS IN THIS CHAPTER

Psychoeducational

SPEMS (page 39): Describes the importance of self-care, and allows the client to brainstorm possible areas of improvement.

Talk-Based

Visualizing the Metaphor (page 42): This intervention encourages creativity, with a possible homework component, that emphasizes focusing and being with feelings of low mood.

Art-Based

Rainbow of Experience (page 46): Through the use of color, this intervention helps the client to explore the range of the emotional spectrum, tying it into physiological processes.

Hands-On

Posturing (page 49): Using different body postures as examples, the client is encouraged in this intervention to notice the inherent energy shifts related to body positioning.

Relational

Energy Movement (page 52): This intervention invites the client to develop a list of various activities that can increase or decrease their energy (and therefore mood) levels.

Group

Get a Gift/Give a Gift (page 56): This activity encourages a group experience of giving and receiving a gift, using acts of kindness to shift moods and motivation.

Homework

Your Future Self (page 59): This intervention allows the client to search for internal resources and motivation for supporting themselves when experiencing low mood.

▶ SPEMS

Type of Activity

Psychoeducational

AMOUNT OF TIME

20–30 minutes

MATERIALS NEEDED

- Paper (optional)
- Pen (optional)

Intent/Used for . . .

The notion of self-care is not unique to this book. Helping professionals talk about self-care in a variety of ways: taking some 'me time,' hanging out with friends, getting outside for a bit, etc. When dealing with low mood and depression, however, it is important to unpack the idea of self-care a bit more. It is sometimes necessary to remind a client of the importance of self-care in managing their symptoms; in fact, self-care is, in many ways, a proactive approach to managing common symptoms of low mood, depression, and even anxiety. This activity educates the client in the basic tenets of self-care, easily remembered by the acronym SPEMS.

Step-by-Step Instructions

1. Explain the following to the client:
   - Self-care underlies healthy living in general, and it is particularly relevant for your mental health.
   - We can divide self-care into five domains. These domains can be thought of as buckets that need filling. We are at our best when our buckets are full, or nearly full, but it takes work to keep them that way. When we are feeling low, or our anxiety is high, it may be because our buckets are low or—in some cases—empty. It is important to look at all five buckets; it's typical to lose sight of one or two of the buckets every once in a while, and these are often the ones that need filling the most!
   - Self-care is unique to the individual. We can fill our buckets in many different ways. Because there are so many ways to fill each bucket, something that works well for one person may not work well for another.
2. For each of the five 'buckets' that follow, discuss possible activities with the client. Invite the client to identify one or two activities that fit within each bucket of self-care, noting which activities they may be able to do over the following weeks.
   - *Social*: The Social bucket is filled through the connections that we have with the people around us. In some cases, our social connections to others are not strong enough, so we need to put effort into planning time to spend with others. On the other hand, we may spend too much time with the people in our lives (our social connections can become overloaded), in which case being able to take some time for ourselves may help to fill this bucket.
   - *Physical*: The Physical bucket ensures that we maintain healthy habits, which can include physical activity, nutrition, or relaxation. Regular physical activity is important—doing something that increases your heart rate at least once per week is a good place to start. Regarding nutrition, aim to have snacks and meals that provide a wide variety and healthy range of nutrients in your diet. Relaxation is a tricky one for many people to balance, but it is important to plan for some downtime every once in a while, to give your body a break.

- *Emotional*: The Emotional bucket is often forgotten. The important part of this bucket is to ensure that you are giving yourself space and permission to feel a range of emotions—both 'positive' and 'negative.' The crucial word is permission. Emotional self-care ensures we aren't trying to bottle up everything negative in our lives, but rather we are giving ourselves permission to experience some of those distressing emotions in a healthy and effective way.
- *Mental*: The Mental bucket is about both activating and relaxing your brain. The activities that can fill this bucket are typically things that make us think, such as solving puzzles or learning a new skill. It is important to note that formal academics may not count as self-care, as the individual assignments and studies are typically assigned by somebody external to the self. Alternatively, letting the brain relax is also important—finding those activities which allow us to put worries and thoughts on hold, even for a few minutes, is also considered Mental self-care.
- *Spiritual*: The Spiritual bucket is about recognizing things outside of yourself. This is often the most difficult bucket to define, as spirituality can mean many different things, and it's important to note that it can—but does not necessarily mean—religion. For many people, Spiritual self-care can simply be getting outside and taking the time to notice things in nature that they don't always have time to notice. Anything that allows you to focus on others or the world around you can be considered Spiritual self-care.

3. Once you have explained the five buckets to the client, note that they form an acronym, SPEMS. Remind the client that they can think about the acronym whenever they are feeling low, and perhaps plan to do something that will fill one of the buckets.

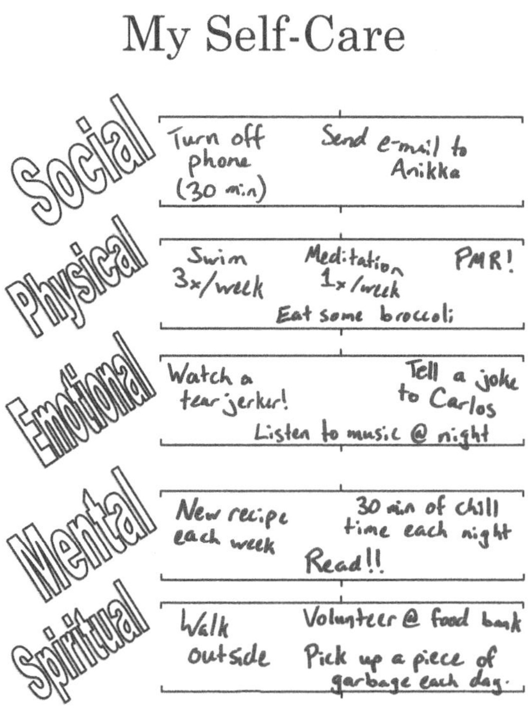

Figure 2.1 A sampling of possible self-care activities that fall under the SPEMS categories.

Guiding Questions

- I wonder how you may be able to fit some of this into your own life.
- How do you know when your buckets are being drained, or are close to empty?
- Knowing what you do about yourself, what helps to fill your bucket(s)?
- I wonder how efficient it is for you to continue going on (working, in a relationship, etc.) without getting some self-care in?

Tips/Ways to Change

- For younger clients, the entire activity/education around SPEMS may not be applicable, as children and youth often do not have as much control over their schedules and free time as adults. However, you can still explain the concept of 'buckets' and how sometimes, when our buckets are low or empty, we can get cranky, and it is important to fill them back up somehow.
- As you are explaining SPEMS, and then debriefing each bucket with the client, it is sometimes useful to have the client jot down their own ideas for self-care so that they have a takeaway.
- It is important to emphasize that self-care does not have to be an all-consuming activity. Having the client commit to doing one small item of self-care, regardless of what it is, can help to spark some recovery.
- Throughout the discussion, clients will often remember an activity that they used to do for self-care and have recently put aside—take some time to highlight how this may be impacting them more than they previously realized.

NOTES

VISUALIZING THE METAPHOR

AMOUNT OF TIME

30–40 minutes

MATERIALS NEEDED

- None

Type of Activity

Talk-based/Motivational

Intent/Used for . . .

Occasionally, when a client is feeling low, it can be difficult to motivate themselves to do a variety of things. Daily tasks become tedious, and the client's frustration can be increased by an inability to reach self-set goals. This activity looks at motivation from a different angle—emotions. By recognizing and reminding a client about their goals in a metaphorical way, the client often can gain a sense of hope that will then lead to accomplishments in other goal-oriented areas of their life.

Step-by-Step Instructions

1. Using active listening, discuss with the client how they see their current experience of low mood (see Guiding Questions for more details on this step).
2. Explain that you will together be using this metaphor for the client's experience and developing it further.
3. If appropriate, have the client come up with a name for the mood or experience that makes it their own.
4. Explain that the experience they have just described could be similar to a movie or a book (depending on the client). Denote this particular description as 'Scene One.'
5. Explain that the next parts do require a bit of imagination. Invite the client to consider 'Scene Three.' In Scene Three, the experience from Scene One has been dealt with or managed. At this point, the client does not need to be concerned about how this occurs, but simply think about what will be changed about the scene and what it will look like once this change does occur.
6. Invite the client to describe what Scene Three could potentially look like—encourage the client to use and build on the metaphor from Scene One. This step does not have to be overly involved or descriptive; however, the more a client can detail Scene Three, the more hope will ultimately be provided.
7. Now that Scenes One and Three have been described, encourage the client to create a potential Scene Two—again, using the metaphor (not real life) to look at what change could be taking place between Scenes One and Three.
8. Once the three scenes have been described, ask the client to identify the emotions that are associated with each scene. Encourage the client to identify more than one emotion for each scene.
9. Invite the client to explain, out loud, Scene One, Scene Two, and then Scene Three. While this is occurring, encourage the client to connect with their emotions that are associated with each scene—giving them space to sit with each emotion, including unpleasant ones.

Figure 2.2 While it is often the trickiest scene to consider, Scene Two is where we find the greatest potential for actionable change.

10. Have the client visualize the metaphor in its entirety (Scenes One to Three) multiple times over the following weeks. Be prepared to note if any parts of the metaphor change, and discuss this.

Guiding Questions

- Scene One:
  - When you picture this mood/experience in your mind, what does it actually look like?
  - What colors are associated with this mood/experience?
  - What actions are being done, by you or the mood (for example, is there 'squeezing' involved, or are you beating your hands against something)?
  - Is the mood/experience seeming like a separate being/entity (a person, shadow, voice, etc.), or is it inanimate (a wall, room, river, etc.)?
  - Does this remind you of another scene/chapter/etc. from a movie/book/etc. that will make it easier to describe?
- Naming:
  - When you think of this mood/experience, what would be an appropriate name for it?
  - Try to have this name reflect accurately what you've just described.
  - Does it make sense for the name to be an actual person's name, or is it the emotion itself? Try not to use a clinical name (like depression), as this doesn't really identify the experience as yours.

- Scene Three:
  - When you think about a resolution, or 'happy' ending, to the experience in Scene One, what might that look like? Not the actual thing that happens before the ending—that's Scene Two—but what does Scene Three look like?
  - Is the mood/experience from Scene One entirely gone, or is it changed in some way to make it 'more manageable'?
  - Are there things that can be added to the metaphor (or taken away) that weren't present in Scene One, now that things are resolved?
- Scene Two:
  - How do we get from Scene One to Scene Three? Remember, right now we're staying in the metaphor, so don't worry about 'real life.'
  - Make this scene really reflect your own preferred genre—so, for example, if you are into science fiction, maybe there are ray guns or space ships. Fantasy? Magic and wands. Adventure? Heroic teams and resources.
  - Remember that we are getting from Scene One to Scene Three—this is a small but important step, so let's really take some time to develop this.
  - What role do *you* have in Scene Two? Are you the agent of change somehow?
  - Where do the tools/props in this scene come from? Do they suddenly materialize? Are they there in Scene One but not visible?
- Follow-up:
  - How was it for you to 'be' with the emotions, not just in Scene One, but in Scenes Two and Three?
  - Did anything change for you about the metaphor while you were visualizing it?
  - I wonder how Scene Two could be translated into real life.

Tips/Ways to Change

- This intervention can be used for a variety of client issues, and is not limited to low mood or depression.
- The naming of the mood/experience can be difficult for a client, especially if they have been accustomed to using formal diagnoses to describe it. This is an important step for the client to become a bit more empowered in their healing process; however, it may be useful to allow the client to take a few sessions before coming up with a new name for the mood/experience.
- Different clients will connect better with different types of story metaphors. Typically, a client will connect easiest with a movie or film metaphor. However, some like to think of the scenes as 'chapters' in a novel, and younger clients may connect better with a video game metaphor—the scenes become levels with boss battles.
- Scene One tends to be the easiest to describe. If a client is having difficulty with this particular step, they may not be ready for this intervention as a whole.
- The most important (and powerful) part of this intervention is the evoking and acceptance of emotions. Typical emotions that clients attach to each scene are:
  - Scene One—fear, helplessness/hopelessness, being trapped, frustration (with self or metaphor), anger (at self or metaphor), boredom, familiarity

  - Scene Two—hope, empowerment, trepidation, confidence, courage, uncertainty
  - Scene Three—joy, relief, trepidation/fear (of recurrence), disbelief (at success), excitement, fatigue
- For each of the scenes, strongly encourage the client to truly visualize the scene in its entirety—textures, sights, and smells are particularly powerful.
- The final step (rehearsal) makes for an excellent homework; however, if the client is struggling with emotional regulation (see Emotional Regulation chapter on page 65), encourage this rehearsal within the session only.
- Follow-up can include describing what the real-world equivalents of the actions in Scene Two may be.

NOTES

▶ RAINBOW OF EXPERIENCE

AMOUNT OF TIME

5–15 minutes

MATERIALS NEEDED

- Paper
- Crayons or colored pencils

Type of Activity

Art-based

Intent/Used for . . .

This activity aims to validate a typical range of emotional experiences. The intention is to orient the client to notice their unique emotional range, affirm the natural rise and fall of emotional experiences, and offer education on physiological experiences of emotion. Through a color visualization, this activity explores emotional energy and can further be adapted to a scaling activity as indicated below.

Step-by-Step Instructions

1. Briefly discuss the physiology of the emotional experience, focusing on 'emotional energy.' Share with the client that a period of intense emotional energy requires a lot of physical work—even if we are being still—and that often what is required is an equal amount of rest after an intense amount of work. Offer examples of instances when the client may have seen this rise and fall. Useful examples may include watching a puppy run around very quickly followed by falling to exhaustion, feeling tense and tired after watching an intense movie, or feeling very thirsty and 'blanking out' after giving a public speech.
2. Invite the client to reflect on these examples and to story their own example of a time when they experienced this 'rainbow' of up-energy and down-energy.
3. Invite the client to create a visual image of their *rainbow of experience* using white paper and crayons or colored pencils. Invite the client to choose colors that they feel connect to their experience, and encourage expanding the discussion around emotions through the use of color. Allow the client to be as creative as desired; if the client prefers to use an arc of shapes or facial expressions, affirm this creative understanding of the rise and fall of emotional energy.
4. Reflect on the experience with the client, encouraging the client to discuss the visual metaphor of the rainbow. Invite the client to explore their own shifts in mood or emotional experience, and whether the client notices any times when they feel their energy rising—such as a positive interaction, or an experience of anger. Explore if these experiences offer any relief to the client, even if they are uncomfortable, from the experience of low mood. Expand this experience to include energy falling—such as the experience of quiet reflection and grounding, or feeling exhausted at the end of a full day. Invite conversation about when these experiences feel comfortable and when they feel uncomfortable, or moments when the rising and falling energy may feel outside of the client's control.
5. A useful response or partnered activity to Rainbow of Experience is the Trigger Log intervention (page 88), or a similar activity encouraging the client to track rising and falling energy levels. Further discussion may include finding a comfort zone within the personal range of experience, or integrating other energy-regulation activities presented throughout this book.

Figure 2.3 Representations of the rise and fall of energy encourage finding points of intervention, while also normalizing the client experience.

Guiding Questions

- Have you ever witnessed this experience with anyone you know? Or with pets that you have had? What did it look like?
- Have you ever experienced this? What did it look like for you?
- Which area on this rainbow feels the most extreme to you? Which feels the most uncomfortable? Most comfortable?
- Tell me about the colors that you chose here. Is there any significance?
- In which color(s) are you still *aware* of your experience and not simply responding?
- In which color(s) do you feel like you are outside of your own control?
- What are some things that someone might see you do when you are on different points of this rainbow? Do you see any entry points to try to 'catch' the energy before it becomes too intense? Or places to ride the intensity?
- Does this information make sense to you? What do you think is important about this?
- How does this fit for the discussions that we have been having about low mood/energy?

Tips/Ways to Change

- This activity can be used to accompany a number of other emotional range/identification activities in this text. For instance, Emotion Word Scatter (page 70) provides a verbal follow-up wherein there is an exploration of the emotional vocabulary alongside the visualizing of emotional energy.

NOTES

▶ POSTURING

Type of Activity

Hands-on

TIME NEEDED

5 minutes

MATERIALS NEEDED

- Open space

Intent/Used for . . .

As low mood indicates a lack of energy, this activity is designed to illustrate how the client can intentionally shift energy through enacting different postures. This activity is best suited to individuals who describe low mood and low energy as being related, or those who are noticing changes in their energy levels along with their emotions or cognitions.

Step-by-Step Instructions

1. Validate and acknowledge the client's experience of low mood. Explore and discuss how low mood feels in the body. Common descriptions of the physical experience of low mood might include exhaustion, heaviness, tiredness, and low desire to move the body.
2. Discuss motivation for relief of these physical experiences. Validate the challenges of encouraging oneself toward physical activity when low mood is present. If appropriate, gently share the evidence that increased physical activity is one of the most effective ways to improve low mood and low energy, while acknowledging the difficulties of participating in physical activity when mood and energy are already low.
3. Describe *posturing* as an alternative to more active physical movement. Posturing is the intentional placement of the body in a specific physical pose and expressing a specific attitude with the body.
4. Discuss a 'depressed' posture with the client—slumped shoulders, head low, neck bent forward. Invite the client to exaggerate this 'depressed' posture. Explore where you feel any discomfort in this posture and invite the client to do the same. While briefly holding this posture, share some of your own observations about your experience in this posture and invite the client to do the same. Notice that this 'heavy head' does not reduce pressure and strain on the back and shoulders, but rather increases it. Notice in particular the constriction of the chest, belly, and lungs. Maybe demonstrate the challenges of taking a deep or cleansing breath in this posture.
5. Demonstrate sitting up tall and invite the client to do the same. Pull your shoulders back and chest and belly open, with your chin up and your head balanced along your spine. In this 'neutral' posture of sitting straight and balanced, explore the differences in balancing the head on the neck and the reduced constriction along the chest and lungs. Notice any shifting or reduction of pain or heaviness, and invite the client to do the same.
6. With these two postures attempted, discuss any shifts in energy, however small. The client may need support in noticing shifts in energy, particularly if the client has been feeling low for a long period of time. Notice if the client's facial expression changes at all, or if you feel any shift in their energy or attention, and name these experiences. Notice if the focus of the eyes change, or if the client's breathing has changed. Share these observations with the client and invite any exploration of these small shifts.

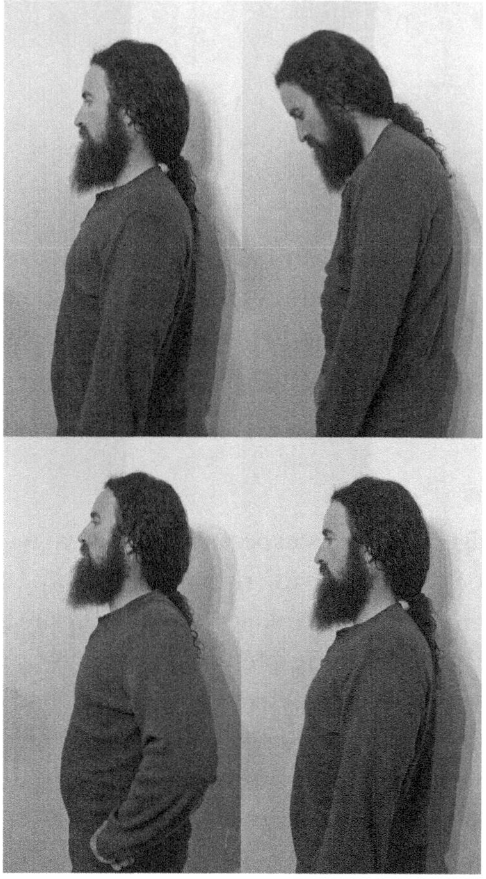

Figure 2.4 Posturing draws attention to the body and how balance and physical shifting can improve mood states.

7. If you would like to continue beyond 'depressed' and 'neutral,' try a few additional postures of your own liking. There are a number of other postures that you can try, or invite the client to share a couple, and have fun with it.
8. If appropriate, invite the client to recall a few notable, powerful, or fun postures. Invite the client to hold one fist in the air, or one finger in the air. Invite the client to hold two fists in front of the chest, as a fighter. Experiment with these movements to the extent that you and the client feel comfortable, continuing to notice how shifting body movements can influence where you feel energy in your body, and how that in turn influences mood.
9. When winding down from these movements, encourage the client to reflect on how they are feeling in the moment. Invite the client to notice any energy shifts that occurred as a result of these small postures, affirming the powerful influence on posturing to energy and mood.

Guiding Questions

- What is it like to intentionally shape your body?
- What do you notice about your breathing?
- Where do your eyes land in different postures? Could influencing what you see influence your mood at all?
- What are some of your 'go-to' postures? Do you have a few that you notice you fall into?

- What is it like to play posturing? Do you ever use posturing in other ways, such as self-affirming in the mirror, or using self-talk to get through something difficult?
- What will you remember from the time we shared today? Does any of this fit for you?
- How does this connect with what we have been discussing about low mood/energy?

Tips/Ways to Change

- One of my favorite postures is a superhero posture: sitting tall, chest and chin out, and fists on hips.
- I also enjoy exploring movement, such as standing with my arms wide, palms up, and looking to the ceiling; I call this 'Catching a Rainstorm.'
- As this activity involves a level of bodily awareness, being mindful of client needs related to body safety is critical. If a person has expressed low mood related specifically to body image or physical pain, adaptations to this activity should be considered.
- Be enthusiastic when demonstrating posturing. The intention of this activity is toward increasing physical arousal; big, open movements are sure to shift energy and attention for the client.
- As with any physical activity, posturing is contraindicative to chronic pain, illness, and injury, and should be used with caution.
- Posturing encourages unique movements and efforts to influence the body-mind connection. If the client is able and willing to consider other body-mind interventions, discussing massage, yoga, or acupuncture may also provide relief through increasing energy and arousal.

NOTES

ENERGY MOVEMENT

AMOUNT OF TIME

10–15 minutes

MATERIALS NEEDED

- Paper
- Marker or pen

Type of Activity

Relational

Intent/Used for . . .

This activity explores energy activators and energy depleters for clients who are experiencing extended or disruptive low mood. The intent of this activity is toward noticing small and subtle shifts in internal energy levels and feeling empowered to enact them.

Step-by-Step Instructions

1. Invite the client to describe their personal and unique experience with low mood, low energy, or depression. Acknowledge and affirm the client's experiences, reflecting on the client's choice of language and clarifying if necessary.
2. Invite the client to discuss ways that they know, from their personal and unique familiarity, how this experience of low mood and energy is different from other experiences. Invite the client to name a time when they felt more energy, or a more lively mood, even if these feelings were only subtle. Note that sometimes a client may compare their experience of mood and energy to someone else, such as saying "I want to be the life of the party like my co-author." While meaningful, encourage the client to connect to their unique energy experiences.
3. Validate the challenges associated with feeling very low in energy and attitude, particularly the feeling of 'stuckness,' acknowledging the additional challenge of being personally responsible for shifting energy states. Further validate the client's pursuit of counseling as a desire to shift this state. If appropriate, invite the client to notice any subtle energy shifts that they have already experienced. For example, feeling nervous about seeing a counselor often results in a shifting energy state. Although nervous does not necessarily mean comfortable or pleasant, this common state offers the client an example of shifting states for the purpose of this activity.
4. Acknowledge that the client may have already attempted a number of strategies to change their mood, many of which may have been cognitive, social, or physical. Introduce the idea of changing the focus from ending the low mood to a slight shift in personal physical energy. Name this experience Activation and Depletion.
5. Define an activator as something that causes—or requires—a lift in energy, such as the given example of nervousness while awaiting the start of the counseling session. A further example of an activator that requires a change in energy is waking up from sleep and opening the eyes—as our eyes take in our surroundings, new parts of our mind and body begin to *activate* and have a sense of readiness, even if we decide to stay in bed; our minds begin to acknowledge colors and shapes, and names of the objects in the room and what they are used for, and this requires new energy.
6. Define a depleter as something that causes—or requires—a reduction in energy. This can be something occurring that requires energy, and so our energy naturally becomes

lowered, such as regular daily activities that leave us wanting rest in the afternoon or evening. Depleters can also be unexpected, such as encountering a person who presents a negative attitude or takes the energy out of a room. An example of an activity that may require a reduction in energy may include entering a sacred space, such as a church, where entering means sitting quietly. Invite the client to discuss any energy depleters that they experience, encouraging their reflection on personal events or activities that they feel cause or require a reduction in energy.

7. Notice with the client if the energy has shifted at all during the discussion of activators and depleters. Invite the client to notice the difference in naming some of their personal activators and depleters. Name if the discussion has slowed, or quieted, when compared to discussing energy activators.
8. Discuss that energy activators and depleters are unique and personal, as each person is unique and personal, and that knowing our personal sources of energy rising and reducing is important. If others in the client's life have been mentioned, offer the example that what one person finds activating, another person might find draining, and vice versa. For example, some might feel a reduction in depressive symptoms from socializing, while others might feel more exhausted after having spent time with people.
9. Invite the client to begin a list of their personal energy activators and depleters. Encourage the client to disregard 'good' or 'bad' judgments while engaging with this activity, as *anger* is a useful energy activator and a fine example for this activity. You may encourage the client to list some of the items that have already been discussed, such as nervousness at coming to counseling.

ACTIVATORS	DEPLETERS
Waiting for counseling appointment	Walking home from counseling appointment
Taking a shower	Reading updates online
Dance class	Listening to gossip
Social justice issues	Too many social justice issues
20-minute nap	1-1/2 hour nap
One cookie	Twenty cookies
Noticing something new	Stack of bills in the mail
Stepping into the rain	No fresh air
Smiling at someone and getting a smile back	Walking with my head down
	Being on the computer all day

Figure 2.5 Noticing small shifts in energy is helpful for choosing activators for those suffering low mood.

10. Affirm the client's choices and encourage a deep reflection of the client's daily activities, particularly small choices that the client makes throughout the day—morning, afternoon, evening, and night—that shift the client's energy. Examples may include taking a shower or drinking a glass of water, two activities that most clients will have a regular knowledge of.
11. Continue encouraging reflection on these small activities, noting how participating in these activities offers shifts to the client's energy, even when small. Acknowledge the significance of small shifts, especially if the client has been suffering from low energy or low mood for an extended period.
12. Encourage the client to engage with this list when returning home. A valuable homework task might be to invite the client to list their daily activities in these columns. Further reflection on how the client experienced the activation or depletion would support deeper insight into the choice of activities, and improve power in choosing an activating activity when necessary.

Guiding Questions

- What are some of the subtle things that you notice when your energy state shifts?
- When is it hardest to notice an energy shift?
- When do you most notice energy shifts?
- At what time of day do you typically have the most energy? The least? What do you think would be different if we had a different appointment time?
- When do you notice you get your ideas? In the shower? In bed right before falling asleep? Or right before waking up? New ideas are typically energy shifts, and they deserve some attention.
- Why do you think we discussed the subtle shifts in energy today? How do you think this might be helpful for you?
- How do you stay motivated when things get difficult?

Tips/Ways to Change

- As a follow-up activity, I encourage the client to identify three things that can be modeled in the next session as energy-shifters, up or down, and I commit to doing the same. This encourages continuity of discussion between client and helping professional, and also allows modeling of shifting energy between client and helping professional in-session.
- If the client is having difficulties identifying energy activators, I will provide an optional activity in-session. Some examples of these include:

  Crumpling a piece of paper into a ball, throwing it into the air, and catching it (or dropping it);
  Bouncing a ball between client and counselor;
  Standing up (vs. sitting);
  Standing up and swinging arms;
  Watching a video of children giggling.
- There are many options to activate energy in-session and to encourage a conversation about this outside of session. I also encourage the individuals I work with to activate playfulness, as noted in some of the creative interventions in this text such as Blowing Bubbles (page 16).

NOTES

▶ GET A GIFT/GIVE A GIFT

TIME NEEDED

5–45 minutes

MATERIALS NEEDED

- Paper
- Crayons or colored pencils
- Magazines (optional)
- Scissors (optional)

Type of Activity

Group

Intent/Used for . . .

Acts of kindness toward others reduce stress and improve self-esteem, in turn reducing the influence of low mood and depression. This activity is designed to encourage a group experience of giving and receiving a gift and to encourage using acts of kindness to shift mood and energy states.

Step-by-Step Instructions

1. Validate and acknowledge that one of the (many) challenges of low mood includes reduced desire to connect with other people, and challenges in activating the best parts of ourselves—such as the parts that are outwardly caring and kind. Discuss how, when we experience low mood and depression, most of our efforts are turned toward taking care of our selves and validate that this is a critical activity.
2. Discuss motivation to shift mood and energy states. Encourage an exploration of the desire to connect with others and to be the 'old self,' and discuss what some of the benefits of the 'old self' are. Highlight some of the 'old self' that is liked and desired by others, or those who may have suggested to the client to seek professional supports.
3. Discuss low mood and depression being an absence of positive emotion, and that the group activity today is a positive activity intervention, where we will work to reduce low mood through showing kindness to others. Research indicates that performing acts of kindness or expressing gratitude shifts the focus from inside to outside oneself. This activity releases the chemical oxytocin, which creates an experience of a positive bond with the person. Giving to others also reduces feelings of fear, resentment, or nervousness that might accompany low mood, and research indicates that people experience moments of happiness when they recall giving a gift.
4. Decide if you would like the participants to randomly exchange images, or use a name draw or a 'pass to the left' method of exchange.
5. Invite the participants to use the supplied materials to create a gift for another participant. Using paper and crayons, markers, or colored pencils, demonstrate drawing a simple box on a piece of paper and invite the participants to do the same. Then, invite the participants to fill in the box with a gift that they believe would support another participant. This can be as simple as words of kindness or as complex as time allows.
6. If you have a good deal of time, consider using magazine images or words, or other craft items such as feathers, fabric, beads, or sequins to create a gift for another participant.
7. When the participants are finished, exchange 'gifts.'
8. Discuss what the experience was like. Highlight the experience of creating, then giving. Then, highlight what it was like to receive something that was created by another participant. Notice any shift in mood states that you observed as the facilitator, and invite the participants to notice any shifts that they experienced. Discuss how activating kindness

Figure 2.6 The act of giving—and receiving—a gesture of kindness creates a slight shift in mood.

can be practiced outside of session when a shift in mood state is desired, and how random acts of kindness or expressions of gratitude might work or not work.

Guiding Questions

- It can be challenging to express kindness when we are feeling something very different. What was it like to move through this range of experience?
- Was it hard to start this activity? Was it hard to finish?
- Did you think about other gifts that you have given that were meaningful? What do you think is the best gift you've given to someone?
- How did you decide what gift to give? Did you use any of your own experience, knowing that some of your feelings are shared by group members?
- Were you more excited to give or to receive?
- What concerns did you have about offering your gift to the group member? Did anyone else in the group have those same concerns?
- What was it like to receive a gift from a group member? Do you feel differently because you know they are going through a hard time right now?
- When was the last time you colored a picture for someone as a gift?
- Do you notice any ways that your attention shifted while you were doing this activity?
- What parts of this activity are you most likely to remember?
- How might you use kindness after this session toward shifting your mood states?
- What are some things that get in the way of using kindness to shift your mood states?

Tips/Ways to Change

- This activity can be modified for those uninterested in arts-based interventions with a thank-you note. Providing stationary and a range of cards for the participants may help move the idea along, as well as offering a framework for a thank-you note being 1) a sentence of gratitude, 2) one example or reason for gratitude, 3) what the writer hopes will happen next or how the actions or events changed the writer's thinking or behaviors.
- This activity can be modified using blank matchbox containers purchased in wedding supply stores. These small boxes can be nicely decorated using markers, paint, or collage images with a small affirmation inside.
- If the group does not seem keen to give each other gifts, anonymous thank-you notes or notes of kindness serve the same purpose. Invite the participants to create anonymous 'love notes' wishing a stranger a great day or a note of encouragement. The participants can leave the anonymous notes in random areas or on car windshields when they leave the building.

NOTES

▶ YOUR FUTURE SELF

Type of Activity

Homework

AMOUNT OF TIME

Explanation: 10 minutes

Debrief: 20 minutes

MATERIALS NEEDED

- Paper (optional)
- Pen (optional)

Intent/Used for . . .

A homework that allows a client to engage in future thinking, this intervention can often spark a sense of hope for clients dealing with low mood or depression. Contemplating the client's future self can also result in a shift in focus from external motivation to internal motivation, which has the potential to create a change in a client's low mood thought patterns and symptoms. This can be a useful intervention when both the client and helping professional feel as though they have 'tried everything.'

Step-by-Step Instructions

1. Begin by empathetically acknowledging the difficulties that the client is currently facing, summarizing any information that has been given around the current low mood and circumstances.
2. Invite the client to share what things, people, or words have helped them to continue up to this point—what has helped them to make it to this session?
3. Give the client a stipulation that this particular homework may be difficult, as it involves thinking, in a limited way, about the future—something which can be challenging for clients dealing with low mood.
4. Ask the client to imagine that it is 20 years in the future, and the client's 'future self' has access to a time machine, something that can be used only once, and the person using the machine is allowed to stay in the past for only five minutes. Continuing the story, have the client imagine that at some point over the next few days, their 'future self' uses the time machine and visits them for five minutes.
5. For the homework, invite the client to consider the following questions:
   - If your 'future self' was here, what would you want them to say?
   - What would you *need* them to say?
   - What would you want to ask them, knowing that they have only five minutes?

Debrief

1. Upon their return for the following session, invite the client to share their homework with you.
2. Discuss with the client why they feel that these are things that they would want, or need, from their 'future self.'
3. Discuss with the client how things would change if they heard these things from their 'future self'—in particular, what aspects of the client's actions and cognitions could change.

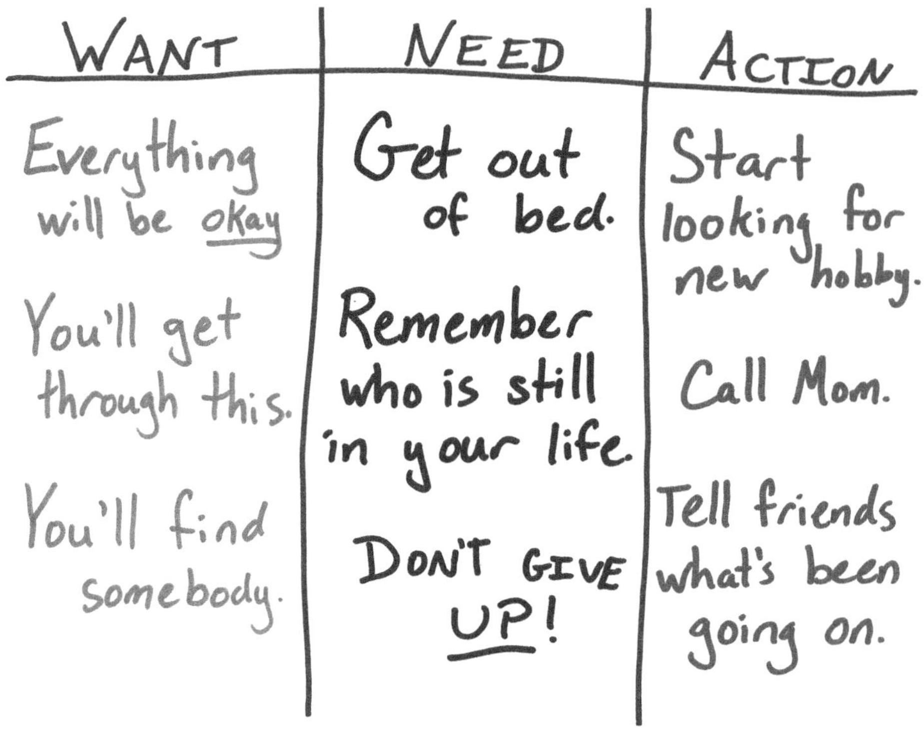

Figure 2.7 Words of wisdom that come from the self, rather than others, can spark a motivational shift.

4. Support the client in developing an action plan for transforming some of those actions and cognitions into reality.

Guiding Questions

- It seems like it's been pretty rough for you—how have you managed to survive? What are you thankful for?
- What type of things have helped you make it to the session today?
- I know the future can be difficult to think about right now, but is it okay for me to give you some homework that involves a bit of time travel?

Debrief

- Why would these be things that you want, or need, to hear?
- What's the difference between those things that you want to hear and those that you need to hear?
- Let's say this actually *did* happen, and your 'future self' told you those things—how would your life change? What would you do differently?
- It's interesting that there's a possibility your 'future self' would have a different viewpoint than you right now—have there been times in your past when you've felt different than you currently do?

Tips/Ways to Change

- Twenty years in the future is obviously an arbitrary number, though one that, for most teens and adults, is far enough away to imagine their life being significantly different. For younger children, lessen the number of years involved in the homework.
- For younger children, the homework can take the form of drawing a scene from the future, rather than thinking about words they would want to hear.
- Most clients will prefer to complete this homework in their head; however, some may find it useful to use a pen and paper to document some of their thoughts.
- The story behind the future self can be adapted to fit the client. For example, rather than a time machine, the client may be more inclined to connect with a story involving spells and magic.
- After completing this homework, the general question of what the client would want or need from their 'future self' makes for a possible way to start subsequent sessions.
- If a client is struggling with the idea of a future in general (let alone a 'future self'), it may be good to open up a dialogue about times in the past when they've felt 'better.'
- Alternatively, the idea of a 'future self' may be too personal, and therefore inaccessible; though the strength of this intervention lies in drawing upon internal resources, it would be fine in this case to use an external/unknown person, such as a 'wizard' or 'time scientist,' who comes back to tell the client something.

NOTES

▶ OTHER RESOURCES

Burns, D. D. (2008). *Feeling good: The new mood therapy*. New York, NY: Harper Collins.

Curry, J. (Producer). (2014). *Evidence-based treatment of depression in adolescents* [DVD]. New York, NY: Routledge.

Jacobs, D. G. (Ed.). (1999). *The Harvard Medical School guide to suicide assessment and intervention*. San Francisco, CA: Jossey-Bass.

O'Connor, R. (2001). *Active treatment of depression*. New York, NY: W. W. Norton & Company.

Sears, R. W. (2015). *Building competence in mindfulness-based cognitive therapy: Transcripts and insights for working with stress, anxiety, depression and other problems*. New York, NY: Routledge.

Segal, Z. V., Williams, J. M. G., & Teasdale, J. D. (2013). *Mindfulness-based cognitive therapy for depression* (2nd ed.). New York, NY: Guilford.

Shea, S. C. (2011). *The practical art of suicide assessment: A guide for mental health professionals and substance abuse counselors*. Hoboken, NJ: John Wiley & Sons.

Teasdale, J. D., Williams, J. M. G., & Segal, Z. V. (2014). *The mindful way workbook*. New York, NY: Guilford.

Williams, C. (2014). *Overcoming depression and low mood: A five areas approach* (5th ed.). New York, NY: Routledge.

▶ REFERENCES

Aaronson, C. J., Katzman, G., & Moster, R. L. (2015). Combination pharmacotherapy and psychotherapy for the treatment of major depressive and anxiety disorders. In P. E. Nathan & J. M. Gorman (Eds.), *A guide to treatments that work*, 4th ed. (463–506). New York, NY: Oxford University Press.

Ahola, K., Honkonen, T., Isometsä, E., Kalimo, R., Nykyri, E., Koskinen, S., Aromaa, A., & Lönnqvist, J. (2006). Burnout in the general population. *Social Psychiatry and Psychiatric Epidemiology, 41*(1), 11–17. http://dx.doi.org/10.1007/s00127-005-0011-5 Retrieved January 16th, 2016.

Allen, J. G. (2006). *Coping with depression: From catch-22 to hope.* Arlington, VA: American Psychiatric Association Publishing.

American Psychiatric Association. (2013). *Diagnostic and statistical manual of mental disorders* (5th ed.). Washington, DC: Author.

American Psychological Association. (2013). College students' mental health is a growing concern, survey finds. *Upfront, 44*(6), 13. Retrieved January 16th, 2016 from http://www.apa.org/monitor/2013/06/college-students.aspx

Craighead, W. E., Johnson, B. N., Carey, S., & Dunlop, B. W. (2015). Psychosocial treatments for major depressive disorder. In P. E. Nathan & J. M. Gorman (Eds.), *A guide to treatments that work*, 4th ed. (463–506). New York, NY: Oxford University Press.

Durisko, Z., Mulsant, B. H., & Andrews, P. W. (2015). An adaptationist perspective on the etiology of depression. *Journal of Affective Disorders, 172*, 315–323. http://dx.doi.org/10.1016/j.jad.2014.09.032 Retrieved January 16th, 2016.

Eisenberg, D., Downs, M. F., Golberstein, E., & Ziven, K. (2009). Stigma and help seeking for mental health among college students. *Medical Care Research and Review, 66*(5), 522–541. http://dx.doi.org/10.1177/1077558709335173 Retrieved January 16th, 2016.

Fiske, A., Wetherell, J. L., & Gatz, M. (2009). Depression in older adults. *Annual Review of Clinical Psychology, 5*, 363–389. http://dx.doi.org/10.1146/annurev.clinpsy.032408.153621 Retrieved January 16th, 2016.

Goldberg, J. H., Breckenridge, J. N., & Sheikh, J. L. (2003). Age differences in symptoms of depression and anxiety: Examining behavioral medicine outpatients. *Journal of Behavioral Medicine, 26*(2), 119–132. http://dx.doi.org/10.1023/A:1023030605390 Retrieved January 16th, 2016.

Jorm, A. F. (2000). Mental health literacy: Public knowledge and beliefs about mental disorders. *British Journal of Psychiatry, 177*, 396–401. http://dx.doi.org/10.1192/bjp.177.5.396 Retrieved January 16th, 2016.

Pratt, L. A., Brody, D. J., & Gu, Q. (2011). Antidepressant use in persons aged 12 and over: United States, 2005–2008. *NCHS Data Brief, 76*, 1–8. Retrieved January 16th, 2016 from http://www.cdc.gov/nchs/data/databriefs/db76.pdf

Ratey, J. J. & Hagerman, E. (2008). *Spark: The revolutionary new science of exercise and the brain.* New York, NY: Little, Brown and Company.

Stolarski, M., Fleulaine, N., & van Beek, W. (Eds.). (2015). *Time perspective theory: Review, research and application.* New York, NY: Springer International.

World Health Organization. (1992). *International statistical classification of diseases and related health problems* (10th ed.). Geneva: Author.

3 Emotional Regulation

▶ WHAT ARE *EMOTIONAL REGULATION* CONCERNS?

Our internal, intuitive, and sometimes instinctive response to our circumstances results in a range of sentiments, defining our emotional experience. This experience can inform our judgments, perceptions, and actions. Often the antecedents and intersection between emotion, behavior, and logical processing is very complex and difficult to define. Emotions work toward influencing our behavior, preparing the body for action via the release of neurochemicals. For example, dopamine release is associated with aggression and risk-taking, while oxytocin release is associated with attachment and soothing (Deans, 2011; Graham, 2013). While our bodies are readied for action through this physiological response, our ability to regulate the emotional response determines the resulting behaviors. When emotional regulation becomes a concern for clients, you may hear this or other phrases explored in this chapter while in session:

"I couldn't control myself; it's not like me to act that way."

As noted above, emotions influence our thoughts and behaviors. Often this is helpful, such as the urge to offer sympathy when a person is upset, or applauding in appreciation. When an unexpected emotion arises, such as surprise or fear, sometimes the behavioral response precludes full consideration of the appropriateness of the response. This is not always disruptive. For instance, consider a mother crying after seeing that her children had cleaned the house while she was at work. Feeling surprise, joy, and appreciation resulted in her immediate but unusual (for her) response of crying. The fullness of her emotions caused her to respond behaviorally before she was able to consider a range of responses that may have appeared more appropriate. This occurs when the overwhelming influence of the emotion has caused *flooding*, which is the wash of neurochemicals being introduced into the brain and body, causing an automatic or instinctual response. Emotional flooding presents in counseling as concerns with self-control or impulse control, especially when the emotional response is overwhelming or disruptive.

"If I don't feel happy or mad, I don't know how I feel."

Common presenting concerns in counseling, such as anxiety or depression, sometimes share an all-or-nothing feature, in that the challenge lies with describing a *range of emotional experiences.* While many are able to categorize experiences into a general pleasant/unpleasant or comfortable/uncomfortable continuum, because the emotional arousal is subtle, a person may not perceive their emotion on a broad range of emotions (Siegel, 2010).

"My stomach hurts every day."

Somatic complaints, such as stomach and head aches, pain in the hips or neck, and unexplained or unusual high energy such as nervous giggling, fidgeting, or bouncing, are sometimes evidence of emotional dysregulation. While it is important for helping professionals to encourage exploration of any physical injury or issue with appropriate referral, it is also good clinical practice to consider connections between emotional regulation and physiological state.

"I know I shouldn't do it, but I just can't stop."

Impulse control with food, alcohol or other substances, gaming, or a variety of other activities often has connections to the ability to internally regulate emotions. External emotional regulators such as these provide distractions from intense emotions and have some short-term benefit. However, using external regulators may have long-term consequences, or result in pathologies such as disordered eating, addiction, or other self-harming behaviors. An enhanced understanding and tolerance of emotional and physiological states improves the ability to connect to a chosen behavior and the behavior's aftermath.

▶ RELEVANCE

Helping professionals have been curious about emotions and their adaptive nature since early inceptions of Western psychology, with William James suggesting a brain-body connection within an emotional experience in the late 1800s (James, 1890). Advances in neuroscience show that James' theory was indeed correct, and as this field continues to expand, approaches toward understanding emotional experiences and emotional regulation have grown beyond behavioral self-control to include body work and interpersonal emotional regulation (van der Kolk, 2014).

Emotional regulation is often tied with many other common counseling concerns. Very high emotional states are sometimes described as anxiousness, fearfulness, or anger, with associated behaviors including mania, over-assertiveness, or hypervigilance. Very low emotional states are sometimes described as depression, sadness, or hopelessness, where a person may present as numb, bored, or exhausted. While a vast range and expression of varying emotional states is normal, when emotional experiences become extreme or persistent, they can disrupt the quality of life. Targeting extreme emotional states through enhancing skills in identifying a personal range of emotion, and enhancing the ability to shift emotional arousal, influences well-being and behavioral control.

As previously indicated, emotional regulation strategies intersect with other common counseling concerns, some of which have been addressed in other chapters. The ability to apply emotional regulation strategies toward intense or extreme feelings reduces experiences of rumination, which in turn can influence anxiousness, depression, and beliefs about identity. Regulating emotions through grounding skills supports health and safety for those healing from a traumatic experience. Emotional regulation skills also correlate with improved executive functioning, support clinical work for a number of pathologies, and may reduce the need for psychopharmaceutical interventions (Berking & Lukas, 2015; DeRubeis, Siegle, & Hollon, 2008).

Self-regulation of emotions has also been shown to influence physical well-being. Researchers at the International Association for the Study of Pain (IASP) highlight relationships between chronic pain pathologies, such as neuralgia, fibromyalgia, and some types of arthritis, to emotion regulation. Further, emotional regulation skills predict adherence to pain management strategies and healing from acute injury (IASP, 2015).

▶ WHAT WORKS WELL

A number of counseling interventions include distress tolerance or reduced arousal as a component of therapy. Many helping professionals would likely agree that these skills are critical even when completing the initial intake session for therapeutic services. The invitation to reduce the intensity of emotional arousal not only offers relief, but also allows the client to focus on counseling tasks and goals.

Interpersonal and socially focused techniques, such as Dialectical Behavioral and Interpersonal and Social Rhythm therapies, highlight emotional regulation through improved awareness of social interactions and modified relational patterns. Decreasing interpersonal chaos by improving social and communication skills, socially focused approaches highlight interpersonal effectiveness, mindfulness in relationship with self and others, and reducing internal criticism. These techniques highlight the arousal cycle, within which our relationship and communication style may poorly influence interpersonal responses, perpetuating feelings of emotional dysregulation. Through the enhancement of skills in identifying desires, as well as communicating clearly and mindfully, these approaches suggest a resulting reduction of external events that influence extreme emotional arousal. Skills work includes awareness of triggers, using mindfulness to reduce arousal, and improved interpersonal effectiveness (Interpersonal and Social Rhythm Therapy, n.d.; Linehan, 2008).

Cognitive and Emotive Therapies encourage reframing evaluative cognitions that influence emotions and emotional response. Skills in identifying emotions that arise when thoughts or events occur, assessing the value of the emotional response, and using different coping and restructuring strategies to transform this response, are all hallmarks of these popular therapies (Albert Ellis Institute, 2014).

Somatic therapies include yoga, outdoor behavioral therapies, and Eye Movement Desensitization and Reprocessing (EMDR). Medically assisted somatic interventions include transcranial magnetic stimulation and pharmaceuticals. These interventions approach emotional regulation through the reduction of physical tensions, intentional release of neurotransmitters, and improved stability of autonomic arousal, which have been connected to challenges of emotional regulation (Felver, Butzer, Olson, & Khalsa, 2015; Jeter, Slutsky, Singh, & Khalsa, 2015; Koperski, Tucker, Lung, & Gass, 2015; National Institute of Mental Health, n.d.).

Across these therapeutic approaches, common themes of emotional regulation include emotion identification, tolerance, and improving the ability to modulate or transform the emotion. Primary tasks of emotional regulation include either to reduce arousal or to increase arousal to a state that allows continued psychosocial functioning. Approaches also highlight the prevention of extreme dysregulation and improving awareness of shifts in emotional state that could result in dysregulation.

▶ FUTURE RESEARCH

Research continues to expand on the bidirectional influence of emotional regulation on cognitions and quality of life; executive function is central to this exploration. An integration of neurological processes and developmental skills, executive function influences planning, focus, and attention. Ongoing research points to the intersection and influence of emotional regulation and executive function. For example, working-memory processes appear to influence arousal and can result in emotional dysregulation; a dysregulated state also appears to interfere with memory functions (Bridgett, Oddi, Laake, Murdock, & Bachmann, 2013; Storbeck & Maswood, 2015; Stout, Shackman, Johnson, & Larson, 2015). This interference is confounded, however, by pleasant emotional experiences. Some emerging research indicates that positive emotions or mood can improve verbal and spatial working memory, while other results suggest that the physiological or cognitive arousal associated with positive emotions may still interfere with executive functions (Gruber, Kogan, Quoidbach, & Mauss, 2013; Storbeck & Maswood, 2015).

Other emerging interests in research exploring emotion regulation highlight the social regulation of emotions, with interesting work being explored on the role of sympathy, community expressions of emotional experiences, and the role of justice-seeking in emotion regulation and dysregulation (Kahle, Miller, Lopez, & Hastings, 2016; Martinez-Inigo & Totterdell, 2016; Reeck, Ames, & Ochsner, 2016).

▶ INTERVENTIONS IN THIS CHAPTER

Psychoeducational

Emotion Word Scatter (page 70): Increasing the client's emotional lexicon, this activity includes an invitation to consider how a range of emotions varies by intensity.

Talk-Based/Motivational

Being of Pure Emotion (page 73): Using the safe space of the counseling session, the client is invited to fully consider an overwhelming emotion and to normalize the experience of that emotion.

Art-Based

Colors of Emotion (page 76): Using visual and sensory cues, the client is invited to visualize an emotional range using colors. The produced spectrum orients the client toward shifting emotional intensity from extreme to settled states.

Hands-On

Pleasant Emotions (page 79): This intervention is an exploration of pleasant emotional experiences, inviting the storying of a range of pleasant memories or events while exploring different arousal states.

Relational

Yes/No (page 82): This intervention is an exploration of shifting emotional states brought about by settling in to the relational experiences of 'Yes' and 'No.'

Group

Fast and Slow (page 85): Encouraging awareness of personal rhythms and connecting shifting energy states, this group activity uses percussion to explore rising and falling energy and group awareness to explore attunement to the energy states of others.

Homework

Trigger Log (page 88): Through tracking the client's emotional range outside of the session, this homework identifies catalysts to certain emotions and builds discussion around a range of emotions.

▶ EMOTION WORD SCATTER

AMOUNT OF TIME

20 minutes

MATERIALS NEEDED

- Sticky notes
- Marker or pen
- Large flat surface (wall or table)
- Digital camera (optional)

Type of Activity

Psychoeducational

Intent/Used for . . .

This activity is useful for helping to give clients a more comprehensive emotional lexicon, allowing them to identify not just where an emotion lies on a spectrum, but also the varying intensity of emotions. It is recommended for clients who have difficulties in this type of identification, but also for when the helping professional is about to embark on any interventions or therapeutic goals that require emotion identification. This is a great activity to start with in the first few sessions.

Step-by-Step Instructions

1. Preface the activity by noting to the client that sometimes it can be difficult to identify emotions; however, it is an important skill in order to address possible emotion-related issues or challenges.
2. Invite the client to list as many possible emotions as they can think of, writing (or drawing) each one on a separate sticky note.

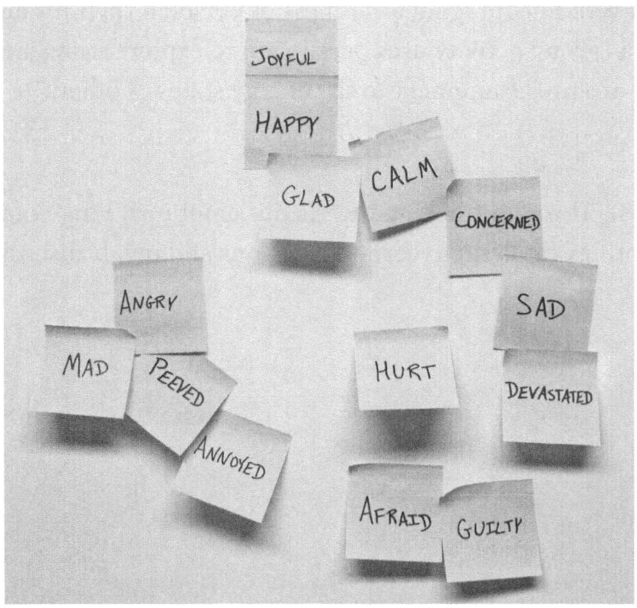

Figure 3.1 Note the unique placement of 'hurt' between 'sad,' 'afraid,' and 'annoyed.'

3. Invite the client to group the emotions that they have listed on a surface (a table works well, but a wall is preferable). Encourage the client to organize the emotions in a way that makes the most sense for them. For example, 'angry' and 'mad' are often placed near to each other.
4. Take some time to discover why the client has organized the emotions in the way that they have—for example, are they grouped by intensity, negativity vs. positivity, etc.?
5. Note any gaps within the organized emotions and invite the client to fill in these gaps as best as possible. For example, perhaps the client has organized the emotions based on intensity, but 'furious' is without a counterpart. In this case, 'irritated' may be a less-intense emotion that could be added.
6. Taking a few emotion words as examples, ask the client to describe how they *know* when they are feeling that particular emotion.
7. Using a predetermined list of emotions (easily obtained through a simple online search), invite the client to add a number of emotions to the table/wall where the client feels they fit best. Remind the client that the purpose here is to increase their emotional vocabulary, so it is okay to take some time before placing a new emotion.
8. Invite the client to ask any questions around what certain emotions, or emotion words, mean.
9. Allow the client to take a picture of or copy the 'emotional spectrum' they have created—this can be taken home, or kept in the therapist's office, for reference in future situations or sessions.

Guiding Questions

- What do you think about when I say the word 'emotion'?
- Tell me a bit about why you organized the sticky notes in this way.
- How do you know when you are (particular emotion)? Where do you feel it in your body? What types of thoughts go through your head? What do you *do*?
- When you say "I am frustrated," does that mean the same thing as when your (partner/friend/colleague) says "I am frustrated"?
- When would you feel (emotion)? Have you ever identified the emotion out loud when in those situations?

Tips/Ways to Change

- Note that some clients may not be able to describe how they know or feel an emotion—in these cases, invite the client to start with describing situations where they have felt that emotion previously.
- There are many emotional vocabulary lists available through a simple online search—feel free to use these or create your own list.
- If markers or colored pencils are available, some clients enjoy using colors to write the words, using different colors or shades to denote different ends of the spectrum or intensities.
- For younger children, it is often useful to have a ready-made emotion wheel that they can then fill in with a few more words—the younger the client, the fewer emotion words you will likely aim for.

- Also with younger children, it is possible to have the client draw the emotion, rather than write out the word. This can be them drawing themselves feeling that emotion, or drawing whatever comes to mind.
- Keep in mind that one of the goals of this intervention is to increase the client's emotional lexicon and vocabulary—ideally, the client will come away having learned at least one new word.
- This can also easily adapt to a homework—invite the client to set a goal for using a set number of different emotion words in conversation before the next session.

NOTES

▶ BEING OF PURE EMOTION

AMOUNT OF TIME

10–15 minutes

MATERIALS NEEDED

- Paper (optional)
- Marker or pen (optional)

Type of Activity

Talk-based/Motivational

Intent/Used for . . .

This activity serves two purposes. The first is to normalize a client's experience of emotion, providing context for what at times may seem to be an overwhelming sensation. The second is to encourage and allow a client to sit in a safe place with an emotion that may otherwise be distressing. This activity can also be used or adapted to instill hope in a client when certain emotions are desired but seemingly inaccessible, for example, when a client says "I'm never going to feel happy again."

Step-by-Step Instructions

1. Invite the client to identify an emotion that is particularly distressing for them—this may require some probing or empathic responses.
2. Discuss with the client the notion that humans in general are emotional beings. We do not often see it on the outside; however, our bodies tend to 'need' emotion. Include discussion about how, even though it sometimes feels like these emotions are in control, it would actually look quite different if they had total power over us.
3. Invite the client to externalize the distressing emotion—what color(s) it is, where it is located in the body—and list any other words or descriptors that would describe it well.
4. Introduce the question of how life may be different if the client *was* that emotion, or embodied it entirely—that is, what it would be like if there were no other controls or influences except for that one emotion.
5. Reflecting on the above responses, invite the client to explore what their life would look like if this were the case—what decisions would they make, who they would associate with the most, what their energy levels would look like, etc.
6. Allow the client space to connect to this possibility.
7. Debrief with the client their ideas around embodying an emotion versus what the reality is about how they live their life.

Guiding Questions

- We all feel a number of emotions throughout our lives—which ones do you feel impact you the most?
- Where do you feel this emotion? Does it remind you of anything? If you picture it in your head, what does it look like? What is your gut telling you about it? Where is it in/outside of your body?
- What would it look like if that emotion truly had complete and total control over your life? What if you 'embodied' that emotion, so that all decisions you made were founded solely in that emotion?
- What would that look like? How would your life be different?

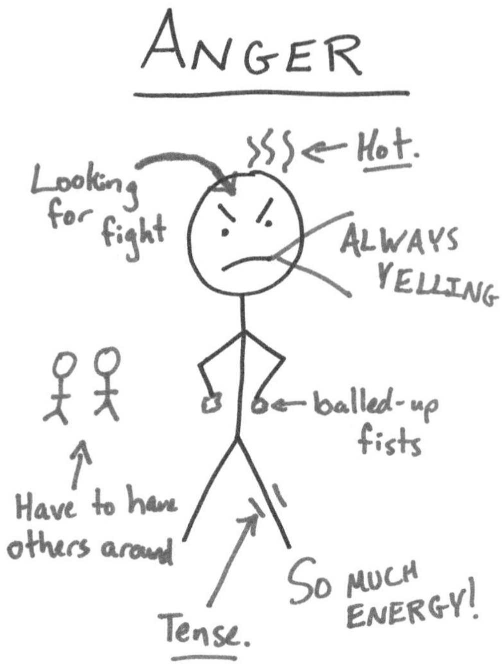

Figure 3.2 The absurdity of truly embodying one emotion can trigger an awareness of other emotions that previously may have been unrecognized.

- What you've just described—your life *as* the emotion—what do you think about this being a constant thing? Is that possible? Why/why not?
- When have you felt like what you just described?

Tips/Ways to Change

- Some clients will have difficulty with the narrative aspect of this activity. If this is the case, encourage them to focus on their gut feeling: what is the first thing that comes to mind, even if it sounds silly?
- As noted above, this activity can be adapted toward instilling hope.
- Have the client identify a desired emotion instead of one that is currently overwhelming.
- Have the client describe and externalize the desired emotion, and also how it would look if they were to totally embody this emotion (similar to above).
- Invite the client to connect with how they felt during this description—could they see it? Feel it?
- Invite the client to brainstorm small steps that they could potentially take in order to move toward this embodiment.
- As per above, it is also important to address that 'full embodiment' of an emotion is not necessarily grounded in reality.
- Encouraging the client to draw (or imagine) themselves as a superhero (for example, 'Captain Anger') is a nice way to adapt this intervention.

NOTES

COLORS OF EMOTION

AMOUNT OF TIME

5–20 minutes

MATERIALS NEEDED

- Paper
- Crayons, colored pencils, or markers
- Paints, chalks, or pastels (optional)
- List of emotion words (optional)

Type of Activity

Art-based

Intent/Used for . . .

This activity aims to encourage identifying and visualizing a range of emotions. Using colors and spatial relations, this activity also explores the personal ability to shift the emotional experience from extremes toward centered and acknowledges the presence of multiple emotions at the same time. This activity was inspired by a behavioral reflection activity in Huber's *How You Do Anything is How You Do Everything* (1988).

Step-by-Step Instructions

1. Invite the client to draw a circle on a piece of paper, then divide that circle into four quarters by drawing an X through the circle.
2. Invite the client to draw a smaller circle inside the large circle.
3. Invite the client to identify two emotions that are familiar. You may also suggest an emotion that has been discussed in-session if the client has difficulty.
4. Invite the client to identify two additional emotions that may seem to balance or oppose those already named. Examples might include anxious/calm, anger/compassion, sad/hopeful, or depressed/hopeful.
5. Invite the client to label the outside of the quarters of the circle with the four emotions chosen. The inner circle is used to illustrate 'centered,' 'grounded,' or 'settled.' Describe the idea of being centered with the client, inviting the client to reflect on being in the midst of emotions but feeling grounded.
6. Invite the client to choose two to three colors for each emotion and to fill the quarters in, representing the experience of that emotion with color. Lines or shapes can also be used.
7. Congratulate the client on completing an original piece of artwork and for participating in the activity.

Guiding Questions

- There are emotions that we sometimes label 'good' and 'bad,' while they are all useful and important. What do you see of that in the image you created?
- Which emotion is the easiest to identify in color? Which was the most difficult?
- Are there emotions that appear more dynamic? More stagnant?
- Do you feel like anything is missing from this circle? Would you have liked to add more?
- When you look at this image now as a complete circle, what stands out for you?
- Have you heard of the phrase 'feeling centered' before? What does it mean for you? Note the smaller circle in the middle of all the emotions—what might this have to do with being centered?

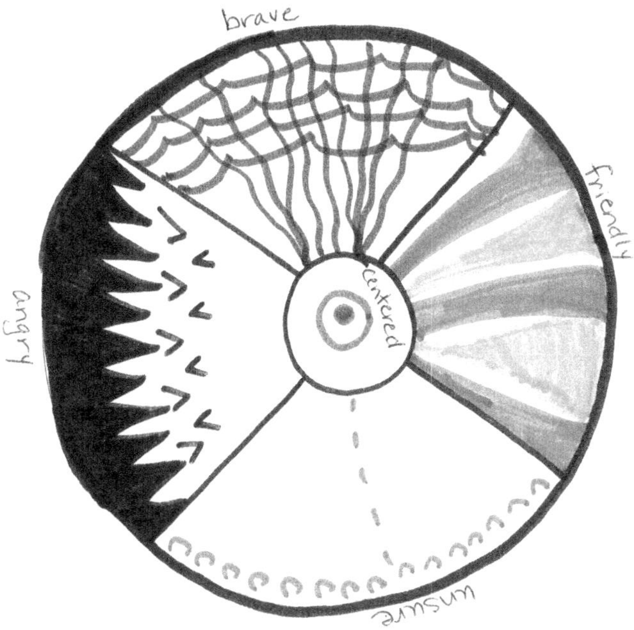

Figure 3.3 The emotions 'brave' and 'friendly' are connected to 'centered,' whereas 'unsure' appears loosely connected and 'angry' is not connected at all.

- With this image in mind, how do you see yourself moving from extremes toward being centered? What do you have to move through or lean into?
- How does this fit with the discussions we have been having about emotion regulation?

Tips/Ways to Change

- The circle can be divided into as many or as few emotions as desired—for instance, six or 10 sections. Care should be taken if the client is expressing, through their body language, attention, or language, that they are becoming overwhelmed by the number of emotions. Sometimes identifying fewer is more manageable.
- If necessary, share a prepared list of emotions, many examples of which can be found through an online search.
- Premade paint placards from the hardware store may be used and sorted into color/ emotion themes, rather than using art materials.
- Circles may be filled in using collage images or colors cut from magazines, rather than using crayons or paints.

NOTES

PLEASANT EMOTIONS

Type of Activity

Hands-on

AMOUNT OF TIME

10–30 minutes

MATERIALS NEEDED

- Paper
- Marker or pen
- Whiteboard (optional)

Intent/Used for . . .

Emotion regulation is often associated with transforming unpleasant or negative emotions, or shifting the extremes of aroused states. This activity invites reflection on the intentional experiencing of pleasant emotions and can provide a space for the client to allow themselves to feel these emotions. This can normalize the wide range of the emotional spectrum, giving the client space to recognize both positive and negative emotional experiences.

Step-by-Step Instructions

1. Discuss the range of the emotional experience, inviting the client to reflect on the full emotional range. Notice if the client focuses on pleasant/comfortable or unpleasant/uncomfortable emotions or experiences. Invite the client to explore why we might focus on one or the other.
2. Discuss the importance of intentionally seeking positive or pleasant interactions while participating in counseling. While this shift in focus can sometimes be challenging, it is important to acknowledge that moving toward an emphasis on the positive can balance some of the emotional challenges of participating in counseling, and can also improve self-soothing and overall quality of life.
3. Invite the client to name three pleasant or positive emotions: one that is expressed or experienced with low arousal (for example, content or satisfied), one that has a medium or moderate amount of arousal (for example, happy or compassionate), and one with a high level of arousal (for example, ecstatic or overjoyed).
4. Invite the client to write these three pleasant emotions down on paper, forming a scale. Together, choose whether this looks like a continuum or another type of scale, such as a thermometer or graph.
5. After the client has written these three words, invite the client to identify further pleasant emotions that may be on the scale.
6. Acknowledge and respect that the client has had a number of pleasant experiences in life that may be overlooked. These experiences might be quite simple, such as eating a delicious piece of fruit or successfully navigating the parking lot, or profound, such as a grand life experience.
7. Invite the client to story an experience which resulted in a pleasant or comfortable emotion associated with low levels of arousal. Acknowledge the client's experience, and reflect on how the client knew it was a pleasant experience and how a low level of arousal was maintained.
8. Repeat this reflection for a pleasant experience associated with moderate arousal and a pleasant experience associated with high arousal.

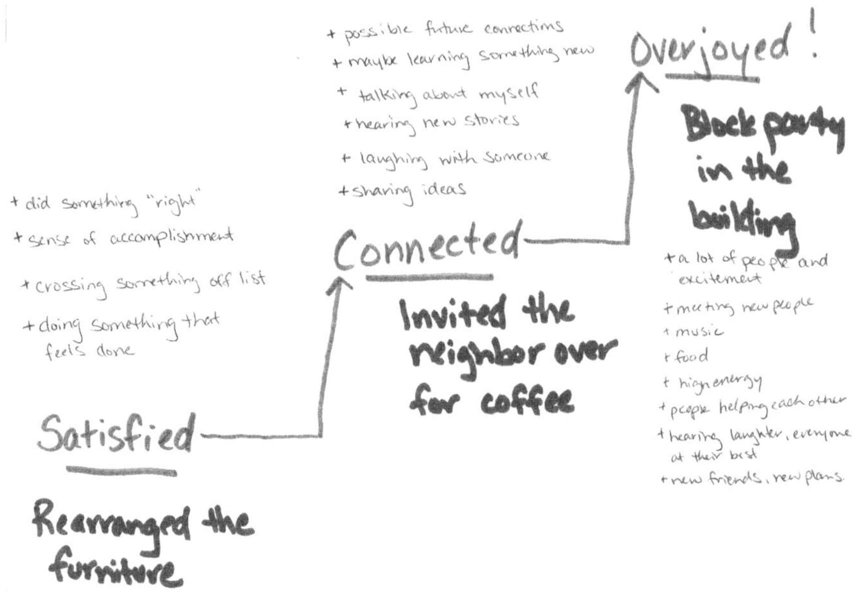

Figure 3.4 Use immediacy in-session: what does the client notice about emotion regulation while discussing these pleasant experiences?

9. Reflect on the different energy states—low, medium, and high—and how the client experienced discussing these different states. Identify any shifts you notice in the client while these activities are discussed. Discuss the intentional action of shifting emotion and arousal states through memory, narrative, and recall.
10. If time allows, invite the client to list a number of activities that result in a positive interaction, comfort, or pleasant emotional experiences. Identify how these activities coincide with the pleasant or comfortable emotions scale.

Guiding Questions

- Did you notice if this activity became easier as we spent more time on it? Why do you think that might be?
- How are pleasant and unpleasant emotional experiences the same for you? How are they different? Consider your body, mind, and thoughts.
- How often do you recall pleasant events?
- Was this activity difficult?
- Is this what you expected to do in counseling today? Why or why not?
- What are the benefits of focusing on negative/uncomfortable experiences? Positive experiences?
- Sometimes people begin to feel as though they 'are' their problem when they come to counseling. What do I know about you now because you shared your pleasant experiences?
- What do you think is the first pleasant emotion you will experience after you leave here? Where will it be on the scale?
- What are you looking forward to?

Tips/Ways to Change

- This activity is well-adapted to the Body Form intervention (page 110), inviting the client to imagine the body's response to feeling a pleasant, comfortable, or positive emotion.
- A pleasant events calendar or journal is a wonderful take-home activity to encourage the client to continue considering arousal and emotional modulation within pleasant events. This has also shown to be an effective protective strategy against depressive symptoms (see Ames, Richardson, Payne, Smith, & Leigh, 2014; Rider, Thompson, & Gallagher-Thompson, 2016).
- When exploring how a client knew the experience was a pleasant one, encourage the client to go beyond "I just knew."

NOTES

▶ YES/NO

AMOUNT OF TIME

5–10 minutes

MATERIALS NEEDED

- Paper
- Marker or pen

Type of Activity

Relational

Intent/Used for . . .

'Yes' and 'No 'are relational words. Used to invite or reject, they can be expressed or experienced on a continuum, such as an emotion scale. Each person has a unique and varied emotional range attached to hearing and saying—or not saying—these words.

This activity invites reflection on these relational words, and also explores the embodiment of this experience. Discussing how these words influence feelings in the body, and also emotional responses to the embodied experience, encourages practice of self-awareness and self-regulation in-session. This practice aims to improve emotion regulation. This activity is adapted from a thought experiment suggested by Siegel in *The Mindful Therapist* (2010).

Step-by-Step Instructions

1. Using a blank piece of paper that both you and the client can see, write the word YES in a list format down one side of the paper, about 10 times. While writing, take time to attune to the client and keep the connection. Maintain an open posture, keep the paper turned toward the client, and encourage their engagement with your writing.

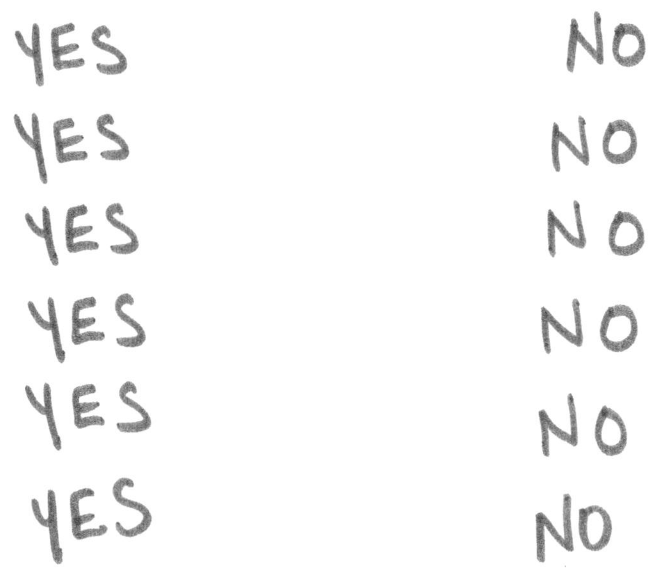

Figure 3.5 What do you notice as you see these words—do you prefer one over the other?

2. Turn the paper over. On the back, repeat this activity, writing the word NO. Ensure that the client can see and experience the visual cue of the repeated word.
3. Invite the client to notice the word NO for a few seconds.
4. Turn the paper over and invite the client to notice the YES list for a few seconds.
5. Invite the client to notice subtle changes in the body or attitude while looking at the YES and NO lists. Invite the client to be specific about where the change is experienced. Stay curious about the client's emotional experience of these words.
6. Notice any physical, facial, or verbal responses that the client might use to acknowledge the list and, if appropriate, share your observations with the client.
7. Invite the client to reflect on their responses to this simple but powerful activity. Most people experience a strong emotional response to these relational words. Invite a discussion on when or how speaking—or thinking—these words influences emotional arousal. Explore whether the use of these words, either to others or to the self, might affect emotional regulation.

Guiding Questions

- Have a look at these lists—what do you notice? What do you notice about you as you are looking at the lists?
- Where do you notice the change you are experiencing? Body? Mind? Spirit?
- Which word feels more powerful for you? Do you know why?
- Everyone has their own unique history with the power (or lack of power) within both of these words. Which do you prefer to say? Which do you prefer the sound of?
- What is it like to say NO right now? What is it like to say YES?
- What images come to mind when you hear the word YES? NO?
- What is memorable about this exercise for you? How does this fit for the work we have done together?

Tips/Ways to Change

- To take this activity further, invite the client to create their own list of YES or NO words.
- This can be an effective calming or empowering activity, depending on the focus of the client and therapeutic goals.
- This also proves an effective take-home activity, as it requires very little in the way of materials, yet it continues therapeutic conversation outside of session.
- Invite the client to illustrate YES or NO to further explore the meaning and impact of these words on emotional regulation.

NOTES

▶ FAST AND SLOW

Type of Activity

Group

AMOUNT OF TIME

5–10 minutes

Intent/Used for . . .

This activity encourages awareness of personal rhythms, using percussive sound to explore mindfulness while shifting energy states. The intentional modulation of rhythms by shifting between fast and slow offers an example of shifting states, improving awareness of shifting arousal. Further, shared percussion is an attunement exercise, influencing interpersonal affect regulation.

MATERIALS NEEDED

- Drums/percussion instruments (optional)

Step-by-Step Instructions

1. With the participants sitting in a circle and facing one another, inform the group that all will be participating in a drumming activity. If using instruments, pass them out, or instruct the participants to clap, pat their knee, tap their chest, or whatever feels comfortable to create sound.
2. The group facilitator should provide the first lead. Invite the participants to attempt to mirror the facilitator, informing the group that you will clap at a moderate speed. Invite the group to follow suit.
3. Begin clapping and allow the group to follow, finding a rhythm. After the participants are attuned to your rhythm, name another participant to lead and invite them to change the speed, if desired. Encourage the new leader to wait for the rest of the participants to find the rhythm.

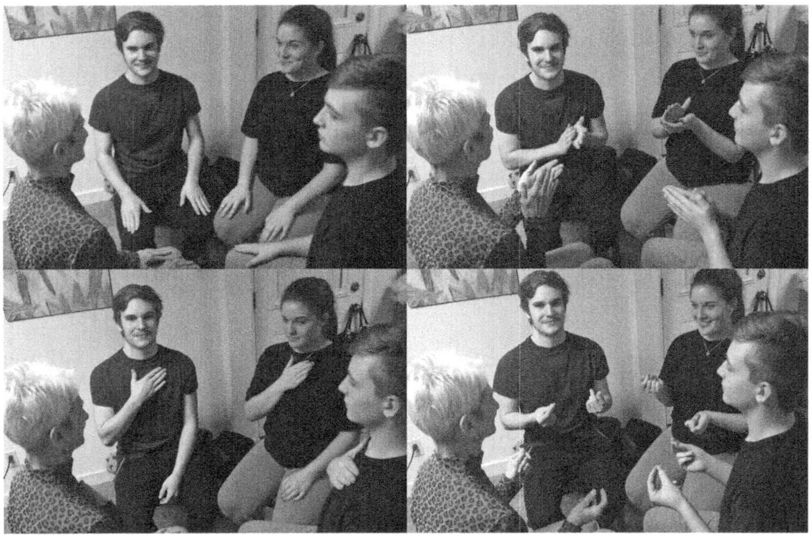

Figure 3.6 Notice and name the shifting emotion states when the group is moving fast, and again when slowing down.

4. When the entire group has settled into a rhythm, invite the leader to name another participant to take over.
5. Continue as time allows, encouraging leads to change the rhythm slightly, or to create a rhythm with an alternate sound, such as a foot stomp or knee pat.
6. Using verbal prompts, encourage changing the pace, shifting between very slow, very fast, and moderate paces.
7. When ready to end the group activity, direct the group to return the rhythm lead to the facilitator.
8. Return to stillness and rest for a moment. Reflect on shifting between fast and slow states and the experience of moderating between fast and slow. Discuss shifting between fast and slow states with emotions. Invite the group to consider which emotions are fast, which are slow, and which are in the middle.
9. Invite the group to consider other rhythms that they experience, and how those rhythms may moderate their emotions. Music or dancing are obvious responses; however, other rhythms include the changing of the seasons or daily energy levels. Social rhythms are also an area worth exploring, based on the desires and focus of the group.
10. Connect rhythms to emotion regulation through discussing levels of arousal when the rhythm is very fast or very slow, inviting discussion on anything that arises for the group members about shifting pace, following or leading, or preferred speed.

Guiding Questions

- Did you prefer fast or slow?
- When did you notice that it became difficult to connect with someone else's rhythm?
- Do you think this activity would look different if you were with your family group? Friend group?
- What would this be like with more people? With fewer?
- Was there a time when you wanted to have your own rhythm?
- What are some of the emotions that have a fast rhythm? How do you know?
- What are some of the emotions that have a slow rhythm? How do you know?
- What about rhythms that are between fast and slow? Can you tell the difference when you are in the middle?
- When is fast too fast? And slow too slow? What is it like in these two states? What do you want to happen when you feel too fast or too slow?
- What does this have to do with emotions? How does this fit for you?

Tips/Ways to Change

- Be aware of any physical limitations the group participants may have, in particular when selecting instruments or activity levels.
- Many percussion instruments can be used for this activity, but tapping on knees, clapping, or patting the chest work equally well.
- This intervention could be adapted to movement rather than percussion. Invite the participants to walk very quickly around the room, then shift to walking very slowly, then find

middle states. Continue with the mindset and intention of noticing fast and slow energy states and shifting between them, and also encouraging the participants to attune with the energy of each other.

- I prefer to finish this activity with hand-on-chest, slowing the rhythm to a heartbeat before bringing the group to stillness.
- Prompts by the group facilitator that ask what emotion should be patterned adds an interesting and creative element.
- An alternate—and advanced—adaptation of this activity includes inviting one or two group members to clap a different rhythm from the other group members. Reflection can include the challenges of regulating our personal rhythm (or emotion) when others are enacting a different rhythm (or emotion). Reflecting questions might explore how to overcome those obstacles, such as shutting the eyes or focusing on a spot on the floor in order to deeply listen to the personal rhythm.

NOTES

▶ TRIGGER LOG

AMOUNT OF TIME

Explanation: 10 minutes

Debrief: 15 minutes

MATERIALS NEEDED

- Paper
- Pen or pencil

Type of Activity

Homework

Intent/Used for . . .

This activity is designed to help a client in recognizing when certain emotions (or thoughts) are triggered. It is particularly useful for clients who feel that their emotions are uncontrollable or spontaneous. Though in certain experiences this may indeed be the case, clients who complete this homework may find that there is more predictability to their emotions than previously thought. For the helping professional, this activity opens the way for exploring emotional regulation in future sessions by enhancing the client's emotional recognition.

Step-by-Step Instructions

1. Begin by inviting the client to identify one particular emotion with which they are struggling—the issue can be one of unwanted outbursts (for example, shouting at a partner), unexpected intensity (for example, crying for hours), or any other concern.
2. Invite the client to consider the most recent time during which they experienced this emotion—ask the client, if possible, to rate the intensity of the experienced emotion on a scale of 1–10 (10 being high, 1 being low).
3. Ask the client to explain what a '1' on the scale would look like, and then what a '10' on the scale would look like. If the client is able to do so fairly easily, ask them to explain what one up or down from the previously discussed situation would look like. (For example, if the experience was a '7,' what would an '8' or '6' look like?)
4. Going back to the most recent experience, invite the client to note any details leading up to the emotion reaching that number on the scale. In particular, focus on the time of day, what they were doing, any words/phrases said or actions done by others, and what their thoughts (or 'last coherent thoughts') were.
5. Explain that the client's homework will look at what triggers may be leading to this 'emotion scale' going higher. Normalize that the emotion itself is very human, and sometimes even makes sense; however, it is the intensity of the emotion that is currently difficult to manage. Part of that management going forward will be to have an in-depth idea of what leads to the intense emotion, allowing the client to possibly react or intervene earlier in the experience than previously thought.
6. For homework, ask the client to record their experiences with that emotion every time they feel it—depending on the client, this could be a one-day log, or a one-week log:
   - Emotion—any words describing the emotion (anger, rage, simmering, etc.)
   - Intensity—how intense the emotion was at its peak, on the 1–10 scale
   - Time of day—as specific as possible, though morning/afternoon/night is also fine
   - What I was doing—where the client was, any activity they were doing immediately beforehand

TRIGGER LOG						
Emotion	*Intensity*	*Time*	*Doing?*	*Others?*	*Where felt*	*Thoughts*
Rage	8.5	6:15pm	Home for supper	—	Face + Hands	Where is he??

Figure 3.7 Encourage the client to look for themes in any of the categories, including the time of day.

- What other people did/said—often the easiest for the client to remember. This column is optional, as there may not be others involved
- Where I felt it—this is used to note where the emotion is felt in the body, not a geographical location
- What I thought—the thoughts leading up to the intense emotion, or the 'final coherent thoughts' before experiencing the emotion

7. After ensuring the client understands the homework, help them to plan how they will best use the log—it can be an end-of-day routine, with the client remembering the days' experiences, or perhaps the client will log emotions as soon as they occur.

Debrief

1. When the client returns, invite them to share their experience of using a trigger log, including how easy or difficult it was for them to maintain the log.
2. Invite the client to share any surprises or themes that they may have noted while completing the log.
3. Discuss with the client any themes that the helping professional notes while looking at the trigger log.
4. Encourage the client to consider how knowing these themes or triggers could be used for managing or regulating emotions.

Guiding Questions

- What, for you, is the best word to describe the emotion you've been having difficulties with or experiencing?

- Think about the last time you felt this emotion—big or small. How would you rate that most recent experience on a scale of 1–10? Why do you say it's that number, and not another one?
- What would a 10 look like on the scale? A 1? What about one up/one down from the number you mentioned?
- Even before you take this homework home, are there any themes or triggers that you think may come up most often?

Debrief

- Tell me what you noticed while doing this activity.
- Which part of the homework was easiest? The most difficult?
- What were some of the surprises? What themes have you noticed?
- Looking at some of these themes and triggers, how might you be able to use this knowledge?

Tips/Ways to Change

- As with most emotional regulation interventions, it is important to have gone over at least a few calming and grounding techniques beforehand. If at any point the client begins to show signs of emotionality to the point of distraction, encourage them to practice one of the techniques before moving on.
- Inviting the client to consider specific details around recent events may not be prudent in every case—it is certainly possible to skip this step if the client is unable or unwilling to do so.
- Depending on the client's background, a useful category/column to add to the log may be 'Food'—in particular, what the client's last meal/food eaten was. This can sometimes speak to potential nutrition deficits or trends. That being said, be cautious if a client has disclosed previous issues with eating or food.
- Some clients may immediately tell you they know exactly what triggers them. In these cases, it is sometimes useful to have the client redirect their 'trigger focus' to internal happenings, such as thoughts and body sensations, instead of external events, such as what others are doing or saying.
- This homework is possible to adapt to smaller children—if this is the case, it is best to have a preprinted blank log prepared, and to encourage the child to log as soon as possible after an incident, ideally with an adult to help facilitate. The final column may be more difficult for children to complete; however, encourage them to fill it in as best they can.

NOTES

▶ OTHER RESOURCES

Burdick, D. (2013). *Mindfulness skills workbook for clinicians & clients.* Eau Claire, WI: PESI.

Diener, E. & Diener, C. (Eds.). (2016). *NOBA: Knowledge evolved* [Website]. http://nobaproject.com/

Graham, L. (2013). *Bouncing back.* Novato, CA: New World Books.

Gross, J. J. (Ed.). (2015). *Handbook of emotion regulation* (2nd ed.). New York, NY: Guilford.

Kassinove, H. & Tafrate, R. C. (2002). *Anger management: The complete treatment guidebook for practitioners.* Atascadero, CA: Impact Publishers.

Leahy, R. L., Tirch, D., & Napolitano, L. (2011). *Emotion regulation in psychotherapy: A practitioner's guide.* New York, NY: Guilford.

Saltzman, A. (2014). *A still quiet place.* Oakland, CA: New Harbinger Publications.

Siegel, D. (2013). *Brainstorm: The power and purpose of the teenage brain.* New York, NY: Penguin.

▶ REFERENCES

Albert Ellis Institute. (2014). *Research.* Retrieved February 17th, 2016 from https://albertellis.org/participate/

Ames, C., Richardson, J., Payne, S., Smith, P., & Leigh, E. (2014). Mindfulness-based cognitive therapy for depression in adolescents. *Child and Adolescent Mental Health, 19*(1), 74–78. http://dx.doi.org/10.1111/camh.12034 Retrieved March 18th, 2016.

Berking, M. & Lukas, C. (2015). Affect Regulation Training (ART): A transdiagnostic approach to prevention and treatment of mental disorders. *Current Opinion in Psychology, 3*, 64–69. http://dx.doi.org/10.1016/j.copsyc.2015.02.002 Retrieved March 18th, 2016.

Bridgett, D. J., Oddi, K. B., Laake, L. M., Murdock, K. W., & Bachmann, M. N. (2013). Integrating and differentiating aspects of self-regulation: Effortful control, executive functioning, and links to negative affectivity. *Emotion, 13*(1), 47–63. http://dx.doi.org/10.1037/a0029536 Retrieved March 18th, 2016.

Deans, E. (2011). Dopamine primer. *Psychology Today.* Retrieved February 16th, 2016 from https://www.psychologytoday.com/blog/evolutionary-psychiatry/201105/dopamine-primer

DeRubeis, R., Siegle, G., & Hollon, S. (2008). Cognitive therapy versus medications for depression: Treatment outcomes and neural mechanisms. *Nature Review Neuroscience, 9*(10), 788–796. http://dx.doi.org/10.1038/nrn2345 Retrieved March 18th, 2016.

Felver, J. C., Butzer, B., Olson, K. J., & Khalsa, S. B. (2015). Yoga in public school improves adolescent mood and affect. *Contemporary School Psychology, 19*(3), 184–192. http://dx.doi.org/10.1007/s40688-014-0031-9 Retrieved March 18th, 2016.

Graham, L. (2013). *Bouncing back.* Novato, CA: New World Books.

Gruber, J., Kogan, A., Quoidbach, J., & Mauss, I. B. (2013). Happiness is best kept stable: Positive emotion variability is associated with poorer psychological health. *Emotion, 13*(1), 1–6. http://dx.doi.org/10.1037/a0030262 Retrieved March 18th, 2016.

Huber, C. (1988). *How you do anything is how you do everything.* Chicago, IL: Keep it Simple Books.

International Association for the Study of Pain. (2015). *IASP Publications & News.* Retrieved February 17th, 2016 from https://www.iasp-pain.org/PublicationsNews/

Interpersonal and Social Rhythm Therapy. (n.d.). *Current Research.* Retrieved February 17th, 2016 from https://www.ipsrt.org/currentResearch

James, W. (1890). *Principles of psychology.* New York, NY: Holt.

Jeter, P. E., Slutsky, J., Singh, N., & Khalsa, S. B. (2015). Yoga as a therapeutic intervention: A bibliometric analysis of published research studies from 1967–2013. *Journal of Alternative and Complementary Medicine, 21*(10), 586–592. http://dx.doi.org/10.1089/acm.2015.0057 Retrieved March 18th, 2016.

Kahle, S., Miller, J. G., Lopez, M., & Hastings, P. D. (2016). Sympathetic recovery from anger is associated with emotion regulation. *Journal of Experimental Child Psychology, 142*, 359–371. http://dx.doi.org/10.1016/j.jecp.2015.10.004 Retrieved March 18th, 2016.

Koperski, H., Tucker, A., Lung, D. M., & Gass, M. A. (2015). The impact of community based adventure therapy on stress and coping skills in adults. *Journal of Counseling and Professional Psychology, 4*(1), 1–16. Retrieved March 18th, 2016 from http://scholars.unh.edu/socwork_facpub/53/

Linehan, M. (2008). *DBT skills training manual.* New York, NY: Guilford.

Martinez-Inigo, D. & Totterdell, P. (2016). The mediating role of distributive justice perceptions in the relationship between emotion regulation and emotional exhaustion in healthcare workers. *Work & Stress: An International Journal of Work, Health & Organisations, 30*(1), 26–45. http://dx.doi.org/10.1080/02678373.2015.1126768 Retrieved March 18th, 2016.

National Institute of Mental Health. (n.d.). *Brain Stimulation Therapies.* Retrieved February 29th, 2016 from http://www.nimh.nih.gov/health/topics/brain-stimulation-therapies/brain-stimulation-therapies.shtml

Reeck, C., Ames, D. R., & Ochsner, K. N. (2016). The social regulation of emotion: An integrative, cross-disciplinary model. *Trends in Cognitive Science, 20*(1), 47–63. http://dx.doi.org/10.1016/j.tics.2015.09.003 Retrieved March 18th, 2016.

Rider, K., Thompson, L., & Gallagher-Thompson, D. (2016). California older persons pleasant events scale: A tool to help older adults increase positive experiences. *Clinical Gerontologist, 39*(1), 64–83. http://dx.doi.org/10.1080/07317115.2015.1101635 Retrieved March 18th, 2016.

Siegel, D. J. (2010). *The mindful therapist.* New York, NY: Norton & Co.

Storbeck, J. & Maswood, R. (2015). Happiness increases verbal and spatial working memory capacity where sadness does not: Emotion, working memory and executive control. *Cognition and Emotion, 7,* 1–14. http://dx.doi.org/10.1080/02699931.2015.1034091 Retrieved March 18th, 2016.

Stout, D. M., Shackman, A. J., Johnson, J. S., & Larson, C. L. (2015). Worry is associated with impaired gating of threat from working memory. *Emotion, 15*(1), 6–11. http://dx.doi.org/10.1037/emo0000015 Retrieved March 18th, 2016.

van der Kolk, B. (2014). *The body keeps the score.* New York, NY: Viking.

4 Trauma and Safety

▶ WHAT ARE *TRAUMA AND SAFETY* CONCERNS?

For the purposes of this book, trauma is defined as an overwhelming and often unexpected event that results in extreme emotional, physical, or cognitive pain and suffering. Trauma is typically associated with a specific critical event, or series of events, such as witnessing or experiencing physical, psychological, or sexual violence, extreme poverty or refugee conditions, or natural disasters (Herman, 1992). A trauma *response* includes the varied and complex symptoms that result as a natural reaction to the trauma experience. Together, these responses are described by Courtois and Ford (2013) as a "biological and psychological survival mode" (p. 3), even while the immediate risk of danger, disaster, or death are no longer present.

A trauma response may also arise for those hearing the traumatic stories of others. Labeled *vicarious trauma*, those who are continually exposed to the pain, suffering, or mortality of others may themselves develop a trauma response. This experience has been described by those who work with trauma victims, such as paramedics and counselors, and has been described by family and cultural community members. Vicarious trauma presents when the suffering of others becomes internalized to the extent that it begins to influence the listener's worldview, subsequently influencing their sense of safety (Duran, 2006; Van Dernoot Lipsky, 2009). The following phrase, and others noted throughout the chapter, is one you may hear from clients presenting with trauma or safety concerns.

"Bad things always happen to me."

A trauma response represents the vulnerability and helplessness that a person has experienced as a result of trauma. This loss of power and safety can persist after the event, interfering with a person's daily life. A *sense of danger,* while a normal response to an unexpected and painful experience, is no longer adaptive for the client as the event has passed. However, common presentations of watchfulness and vigilance often accompany a trauma response, resulting in extreme arousal states. This ongoing experience can result in emotional, cognitive, and physical discomfort (Blaustein & Kinniburgh, 2010; Courtois & Ford, 2013).

"I can't stop thinking about it."

Rumination and *nightmares* are common trauma responses. Ruminating is the repetition of a situation or scenario in the mind, without the conscious or logical desire to continue thinking about the situation. Nightmares often share these characteristics, where unwanted images or memories of the traumatic experience will replay while sleeping. While some retrospection of a fearful scenario is normal in that it helps us to make sense of the event, rumination and nightmares after a traumatic event can result in emotional and physiological arousal beyond what is typically associated with a memory (US Department of Veterans Affairs, 2015).

Flashbacks and *dissociation* are extreme forms of rumination. A flashback is an unwanted trauma memory that overwhelms the senses to the extent that the victim re-experiences the psychological, emotional, or physical effects of the trauma. Dissociation includes an element of altered reality or de-personalization, such as seeing oneself as if in a dream, or having an experience of watching oneself from the outside. It is important to recognize that dissociation has been identified as a safety strategy both during and after a traumatic experience, primarily as a means of escaping from suffering where no other coping strategy can be effective. However, dissociation often proves extremely challenging for clients, as it can result in a shift in conscious awareness that is out of the client's control. Consultation and trauma-informed expertise and supervision are necessary for this very specific and challenging presenting concern.

"I don't know how to let people in, and I'm not sure I want to."

Individuals who have experienced trauma have had cause to feel physically, emotionally, or socially unsafe, sometimes by those who have been trusted or are in positions of power. A common response to these types of traumas is *withdrawing interpersonal trust* from all relationships. While protective in some respects, withdrawing trust also results in troubling relationships and isolation. Social withdrawal is also a form of avoidance, which could perpetuate rumination and enhance the fear response, rather than offer any relief for the client (Banks, 2006). Trauma results in a sense of loss of what is known, familiar, and expected. Working with clients toward developing their personal definition of safety and exploring relationships that are 'safe enough' may reduce the influence of isolation, withdrawal, and hypervigilance on daily interactions (Blaustein & Kinniburgh, 2010).

"It is my fault; I should have known better."

Many survivors of trauma express some level of *self-blame, guilt,* or *shame* attached to their experiences. Some may express feeling 'marked' for trauma, or alternatively they may internalize the negative experience as punishment for wrongdoing (Blaustein & Kinniburgh, 2010; Herman, 1992). Further, societal messages about responsibility, such as messaging about walking alone at night or dressing a certain way, enhance the perception of responsibility for the traumatic event (Bouson, 2010). While the survivor may feel empowered toward actions of personal safety, this sense of personal responsibility can become disruptive when resulting in self-blame, guilt, and shame. In discussing healing from trauma and establishing safety, encouraging conversations toward reducing self-blame by acknowledging the blame of the perpetrator is critical, with this conversation validating the client's desire to make sense and order of their experience and the trauma response.

▶ RELEVANCE

It is more likely for a person to seek therapy for a trauma *response* than to process the traumatic event specifically. The disclosure of a traumatic experience may not occur between client and counselor. However, being mindful that a traumatic experience might underlie the presenting concern is important, as trauma is largely overlooked or misdiagnosed (Complex Trauma Task Force, 2012; National Institute of Mental Health, 2016;). As part of a large-scale study across the United States, the National Center for PTSD estimates that as many as 71% of children and youth between 2–17 years old had been exposed to victimization incidents, with 70% of those experiencing multiple traumatic events. Further, the center estimates that approximately 55% of adults will experience a traumatic event in their adult lives. While few of these experiences result in clinical pathology (for example, PTSD or Borderline Personality Disorder), there is a high likelihood that varied presenting concerns may be the result of exposure to a traumatic incident (NIMH, 2016; US Department of Veterans Affairs, 2015).

▶ WHAT WORKS WELL

Judith Herman offered a pivotal work with *Trauma and Recovery* (1992), introducing phases of trauma healing to include safety, remembrance, mourning, and reconnection with the present. These phases have provided a framework for therapeutic best practices across domains, and heavily influence ongoing developments in trauma-informed counseling. Remembrance, mourning, and reconnection are associated with trauma processing, and include exploration of the range of unacknowledged emotions attached to the trauma experience, as well as further integration of these feelings and responses into the present sense of self. The goals across these phases include improved emotional regulation attached to the specific trauma incident, such as identifying experiences of grief and loss, changes to values or ideas about one's identity, and connecting with personal strengths, resilience, and advocacy.

While processing is a relevant phase of healing, safety is considered the primary goal within trauma work and is a main focus of this chapter. Safety goals are not connected with processing the trauma directly; however, the skills developed in this area prove to support improved quality of life and reduced intensity of symptoms related to the trauma response (Courtois & Ford, 2013; Herman, 1992).

Practitioners at the Trauma Center at Justice Resource Institute have developed a number of relational, somatic, and cognitive approaches to reducing the influence of the trauma response. Relational approaches include defining and practicing personal boundaries, using attunement and empathy to reduce emotional arousal, and intentionally establishing the safe space of a client-counselor relationship to explore safety-in-relation. Through interpersonal and narrative approaches, relational counseling aims to reconnect the client to a sense of personal agency and safety, while exploring the loss of what was known and familiar (Banks, 2006; Graham, 2013; van der Kolk, 2006).

Somatic Trauma Therapy focuses toward identifying where the physiological imprint of trauma is held in the body, and soothing and releasing those areas. Body work may include Trauma-Sensitive Yoga (TSY), where clients are invited to improve body awareness and identify power and control in movement. David Emerson (2015), a lead theorist in somatic approaches and TSY, posits that trauma results in a sense that bodily safety is out of one's personal control. Through controlling movement, identifying personal limits, and mindfully shifting and releasing postures, a client can shift toward an improved sense of personal agency, a reduced physiological trauma response, and an enhanced sense of safety (see also Emerson & Hopper, 2011; Ogden, Minton, & Pain, 2006; Rothschild, 2000).

Cognitive approaches to trauma and safety concerns include the use of psychoeducation, mindful awareness, and cognitive strategies to ground clients in the present. Trauma-Focused Cognitive Behavioral Therapy (TF-CBT) has been described as effective for reducing the influence of the trauma response, particularly for associations with a critical event, such as natural disaster or military involvement. TF-CBT components include normalizing the symptoms and experiences of the client through education on the trauma response, and gradual exposure and desensitization to triggering material (Nilamadhab, 2011; Rowe, 2016). There is mixed evidence regarding the application of TF-CBT to trauma related to interpersonal violence, such as sexual assault and abuse, with researchers suggesting to integrate physiological and relational models with elements of cognitive approaches such as this (Cusack et al., 2016; Qi, Gevonden, & Shalev, 2016).

The Attachment-Regulation-Competency (ARC) model of reducing traumatic symptoms integrates relational, somatic, and cognitive approaches, some of which are described above. Exploration of relational safety, emotion identification, and self-regulation, as well as personal agency and identity, are highlights of this model, with research indicating success when using the ARC model for both individuals and groups (Ford & Blaustein, 2013; Kinniburgh & Blaustein, 2005).

▶ FUTURE RESEARCH

There is a growing body of work in the use of non-dialogic approaches to reducing the trauma response. The National Clearinghouse on Families and Youth highlights the use of creativity and expressive therapies such as music, art, and movement to reduce cognitive and emotional arousal, while improving expression of and understanding of the trauma response (Family & Youth Services Bureau, n.d.). Further, as the use of neural imaging continues to advance, art and movement therapies are proving to influence sensory, perception, attachment, and affect centers, all connected to safety and the trauma response (Hass-Cohen & Findlay, 2009; Lusebrink, 2004).

The intersection of social, interpersonal, and individual characteristics influencing trauma and safety has resulted in growing interest in Trauma-Informed Community Building (TICB). TICB acknowledges the traumatic strain of poverty, historical oppression, and violence, which result in a lack of trust and disconnection with community development. Integrating intentional strategies to promote social cohesion, improve information sharing, and reduce chaos, TICB aims to recognize the influence of historical trauma on barriers to community health and development. TICB initiatives aim to improve access engagement in democratic processes, access to social services, and housing and education in historically underserved communities (Weinstein, Wolin, & Rose, 2014).

▶ INTERVENTIONS IN THIS CHAPTER

Psychoeducational

Know Your Brain (page 101): This intervention is a simplified explanation of how trauma can impact the brain and automatic thinking, helping to normalize many of the client's feelings.

Talk-Based/Motivational

Society and Feelings (page 104): This intervention invites critical thinking about social and cultural responses to emotions and how this might influence our feelings.

Art-Based

Shield and Wand (page 107): This intervention is an exploration of the definition of safety through the metaphor of a shield and discussion of personal tools toward safety through the metaphor of a wand.

Hands-On

Body Form (page 110): In this intervention, a body outline is used to visualize embodied safety and practice with shifting arousal states in-session.

Relational

Attuning to the Safety of Others (page 114): This intervention uses body awareness to enhance feelings of calm by introducing the idea of attuning to the physical settledness of another person, known or unknown.

Group

Self-Gratitude Brainstorm (page 117): In this intervention, the group brainstorms the multitude of ways that the body is powerful, secure, and strong.

Homework

Choice Log (page 120): This simple homework emphasizes searching for power and control within the client's life.

▶ KNOW YOUR BRAIN

Type of Activity

Psychoeducational

Intent/Used for . . .

This psychoeducational intervention offers the client information on the impact of trauma and trauma healing on cognitive, emotional, and physical brain processes. The aim of this intervention is to normalize the client's experience, as well as to encourage the client to collaborate in approaches to reduce the trauma response. This intervention proves helpful in setting the stage in initial sessions, as it provides context around the phases of trauma counseling and the focus on safety.

AMOUNT OF TIME

10–15 minutes

MATERIALS NEEDED

- Paper
- Pen or pencil
- Whiteboard (optional)
- Dry-erase markers (optional)

Step-by-Step Instructions

1. Begin by reminding the client that the word 'trauma' is often confusing. Emphasize that trauma is unique, in that a trauma response results in our mind and body interpreting safety and danger. A trauma response can occur from a physical experience of danger, or an emotional or psychological experience of danger, such as bullying or family fighting.
2. Using a piece of paper or whiteboard, draw three boxes or circles. Explain that you will be sharing some information about how the brain processes events and trauma to help the client gain a better understanding of what is going on.

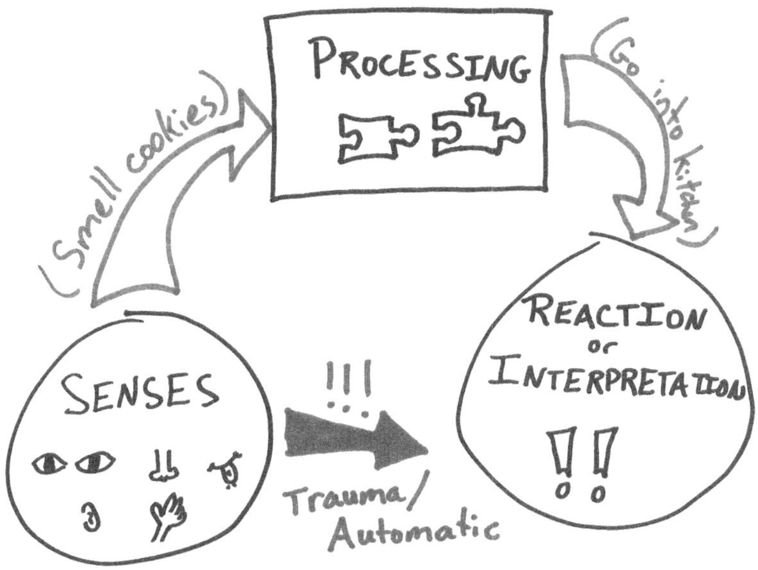

Figure 4.1 A simplified awareness of how information is processed in the brain can be useful in contextualizing subsequent therapeutic work.

3. Label the first box 'senses,' the second box 'processing,' and the third box 'interpretation/reaction.'
4. Explain to the client that sensory information is first taken in from the outside world. An example of this is seeing and hearing rain begin to fall outside.
5. Draw an arrow from the first box (senses) to the second box (processing), in order to denote the typical pathway through the brain (see Figure 4.1 as an example).
6. Explain to the client that after this information enters into the brain, it is then processed. Continuing with the same example, the rational/logical part of our brain notes that if we go outside without protection, we will get wet. Within the same step, it is important to note that the emotional part of the brain also gets a say—for example, there may be frustration about not wanting to get wet as well.
7. Draw an arrow from the second box (processing) to the third box (interpretation/reaction), in order to denote the typical pathway through the brain (see Figure 4.1 as an example).
8. Finally, explain that the brain decides upon a course of action. In the raining example, we may decide to put on a rain jacket or use an umbrella. Note that the reaction does not always have to be overt—it may be more internal or interpretive (for example, a thought might arise that the weather forecaster was wrong).
9. After checking with the client to confirm understanding so far, walk through an example where the brain will typically skip over the processing box. A possible example of this is when our hand accidentally rests on a hot stove element—the brain does not wait for processing, but rather skips to the reaction box.
10. Allowing space for the client to interpret why this reaction may be, come to the conclusion that this second pathway is essentially a 'survival mode' for the brain, and very useful and natural when there are threats in our lives.
11. Explain to the client that a survival mode can also be triggered, and enhanced, through intense emotional, sensory, or environmental situations. Remind the client that these situations can also be referred to as trauma.
12. Using the drawing, emphasize that, with trauma, the brain not only goes into automatic survival mode, but the resulting pathway, which skips processing, is almost immediately strengthened into a strong connection. This can result in certain sensory or environmental stimulation eliciting very automatic responses, which are sometimes seemingly unwarranted or unwanted.
13. Invite the client to reflect on this information and, if desired, discuss if this fits their experience. Invite the client to identify possible automatic or unwanted reactions, or potential triggers for this pathway.
14. Discuss the client's goals for therapy, including re-establishing the connections and pathways to reduce both the suffering around the trauma memory and the trauma response itself.

Guiding Questions

- When I say the word trauma, what does that word mean for you?
- Tell me about a time when you reacted automatically (apart from a trauma response) to something. Why do you think your body does that?

- What might be an advantage to your body/brain going into survival mode with these sensory/environmental triggers?

Tips/Ways to Change

- This intervention can still be appropriate for younger children. Feel free to use different words or terms that fit best for the client, such as 'the mechanic' or 'the puzzler' instead of 'processing.'
- As much as possible, try to use examples to which the client can relate. If the client has never experienced putting their hand on a stove element, explore alternate examples of an automatic response. Care should be taken in discussing relatable or generic examples, particularly if the client has experienced a recent physical or sensory traumatic event.
- The drawing can get quite messy with the number of lines and arrows going back and forth—this is okay, and can sometimes add some needed levity to a session, as the client can likely relate to this sense of overwhelm.
- It can be useful to have the diagram to refer back to for future interventions or sessions. Keep this in mind when choosing materials (for example, whiteboard or paper).

NOTES

SOCIETY AND FEELINGS

AMOUNT OF TIME

10–15 minutes

MATERIALS NEEDED

- None

Type of Activity

Talk-based/Motivational

Intent/Used for . . .

This intervention is aimed toward encouraging the client to consider the messages that they have received throughout their lives about experiencing emotions. Many facets of counseling are about identifying and accepting a range of emotional experiences, learning to regulate and transform emotions when necessary. Discussing ways we self-validate, or invalidate, our emotions, how our response to emotions can cause new emotions, and how we have learned much of this from messages we receive from family, friends, and culture, encourages critical thinking about how a response to emotions might reduce the intensity of the emotional experience. Finally, thinking about social and cultural responses to feelings may enhance empathy and compassion, which are linked to resilience.

Step-by-Step Instructions

1. Begin by discussing the client's unique emotional experience, either with examples from what the client has shared or what has been discussed or observed in-session.
2. Validate the challenges of being nonjudgmental when noticing a range of emotional experiences. There are many examples of these challenges common in Western culture, inherent in phrases such as 'boys don't cry' or 'it is not nice to get angry.' Further discussion might include cultural values on staying positive, or 'fake it 'til you make it.'
3. Encourage the client to discuss messages about emotions that have been received from others in their lives, or society at large. What are the client's beliefs about emotions? Are there 'right' and 'wrong' emotions?

Figure 4.2 We learn from family, friends, and our environment that some emotions may be 'right' or 'wrong,' while all emotions have an important purpose.

4. Explore these experiences with the client, inviting the client to question some of the boundaries of these social rules about emotions. Invite the client, if possible, to notice emotions while withholding judgment, or withholding the impulse to change that experience. This is quite difficult; however, it is an important observation.
5. Introduce the fairly complex notion that having judgment about emotions can sometimes elicit new and more complicated feelings. Discuss how this may add to the intensity of the emotional experience. Examples of this experience may include guilt after feeling anger, or shame after feeling sad.
6. Invite the client to explore any connections or insight that may arise from this discussion, using examples from their own life.
7. Gently challenge the client to consider how these rules or judgments about emotions influence the size or intensity of the emotion.
8. Discuss with the client that emotions have a purpose, like a good friend trying to get our attention about something, but that sometimes the friend can give a little push. Invite the client to consider what a specific emotion might want, how that might be influencing the client's actions or decisions, and how the need might be better addressed. Support the client by starting with some easy connections:
   - Sadness wants soothing. Try hand-on-heart for a slow count of seven, or use the senses to soothe by imagining a scent that feels like home to you, or touching something soft, such as a blanket or stuffed toy.
   - Anxiety wants safety. Look around the room at all of the things that are protecting you in the office (for example, the roof, the door, the exit, the sweater you are wearing).
   - Anger wants action. Notice what the anger is trying to enact and express the opposite. Enact kindness, or move to avoid danger. If this feels impossible, try rubbing your hands together very quickly to a slow count of 10.
9. Explore ways that the client can self-validate emotions, or how the client can think critically about ways that we obstruct a range of emotional expressions on a sociocultural level, and how the messages might be counteracted.
10. Explore nonjudgmental statements about emotions, such as:
    - It's okay that I feel this way.
    - This is a natural human emotion.
    - It makes sense that I would feel this.
    - Everyone feels this way sometimes.

Guiding Questions

- When someone says 'settle down,' does that actually help you to settle down?
- Are there times when you believe your emotions are valid but someone else does not?
- What is the difference between *feeling* an emotion and *expressing* an emotion?
- Sometimes we want to ignore or push away emotions like anger and anxiety. Is there a time that you tried to ignore or push away these big emotions? How did it go?
- What are some soothing, safety, or action-oriented things you can do when your big emotions are trying to get your attention?
- How do/have you defended yourself when someone tells you to 'get over it'?

- What are some self-validations that you already use?

Tips/Ways to Change

- The film *Inside Out* (Lasseter, Docter, & del Carmen, 2015) is being used in schools to discuss the influence of emotions and social values of a range of emotional responses. Clients can be directed to watch this, or other similar films, as a fun homework related to this intervention.
- Martin Luther King, Jr., in his *Letter from Birmingham Jail* (King, 1963), wrote beautiful prose indicating that bringing tension to the conversation does not mean the person caused the tension:

  > We who engage in non-violent direct action are not the creators of tension.
  > We merely bring to the surface the hidden tension that is already alive.
  > We bring it out in the open where it can be seen and dealt with.
  >
  > (para. 20)

  This offers an excellent take-home activity for a client to consider how naming a problem does not make one responsible for creating the problem.
- This activity can be adapted to an art expression by inviting art creation of different emotional experiences, exploring what that emotional creation *wants* from the client, or what that emotional creation *gets* from the client.

NOTES

SHIELD AND WAND

Type of Activity

Art-based

AMOUNT OF TIME

10–25 minutes

MATERIALS NEEDED

- Paper
- Crayons, colored pencils, or markers

Intent/Used for . . .

This activity allows the client to explore and visualize what elements of their lives could be safe and protective through the use of a shield metaphor. The addition of a wand metaphor adds an offensive component to the protection.

Step-by-Step Instructions

1. Discuss the use of a shield as a defense. This metaphor can be discussed in relation to battle, or for different types of strong weather, if you would prefer to discuss something more general. In both historical and current contexts, shields not only offer physical protection, but they also show symbols for what we believe is protective, such as a coat of arms, a flag, or religious symbols.
2. Invite the client to design their own shield on paper, offering examples if necessary. Discuss the creation of a shield that both offers protection and symbolizes the client's source of strength, persistence, and resilience. Using language that suits the age and presentation

Figure 4.3 Protective concepts might include cultural symbols, self-affirmations, safe spaces, or safe people.

of the client, encourage representation of how the client is protected by this shield, literally and symbolically.

3. If appropriate and time permitting, invite the client to also design and draw a wand (or other offensive tool). Discuss that offensive tools are not all-powerful, but rather work with the intention and guidance of the wielder. Consider one or two common actions a wand could complete, such as shape-shifting or invisibility, that could offer additional protection.
4. Explore these two metaphors. Discuss if any pieces of this metaphor are enacted in the client's daily life, or perhaps in the counseling session.
5. Further discussion may explore how these elements have been protective in the past, or how they will serve future needs.

Guiding Questions

- One of the reasons that ancient armies used things like Coats of Arms was not only to identify who they were fighting, but also to try to intimidate opposing armies. Does this fit at all for what you might be battling?
- If you were behind this shield, would you want anything on the back side of the shield to remind you of what was on the front?
- How big or small is this shield? Is this shield heavy or light for you? How do you hold it and what parts of your body would it cover?
- Would your shield have any sort of magic powers beyond defending you in an attack? (For example, some superheroes use their shields as a defense, offense, or even transportation.)
- What else comes up for you as you create this shield? In your mind, what does the use of this shield look like? Can you show the posture? If yes, what do you notice about yourself in this posture?
- How do you know these things protect you? Have they protected you in the past?
- How do you remember these things about yourself when times are the hardest?

Tips/Ways to Change

- Know the client. This activity may not be welcomed by a client who is not interested in metaphor.
- Care should be taken when discussing offensive tools, as they can quickly become weapons. A wand or 'magic power' is a tool meant to access the client's intentional strength and sense of purpose, whereas a weapon may be misunderstood as something with which to harm another or seek revenge.
- Other useful metaphors for discussing safety include a helmet or suit of armor.
- I often offer visual images of shields or breastplates on suits of armor from ancient battles, but typically find that both youth and adults have engaged in popular media to the extent that they can connect with this metaphor—recent examples are *Game of Thrones* (a television program) and *Clash of Clans* (a game).
- With younger clients, you might want to provide the outline of a shield. Older clients may want to create their own shape of a shield, such as a circle or triangle.

NOTES

BODY FORM

AMOUNT OF TIME

10–25 minutes

MATERIALS NEEDED

- Paper
- Pen or pencil
- Whiteboard (optional)
- Dry-erase markers (optional)

Type of Activity

Hands-on

Intent/Used for . . .

This hands-on activity works toward enhancing the experience of bodily control and safety in the present. It includes mindful awareness of the present state of the body, moving toward a discussion of mindfully shifting states. A paper form is used on which body awareness is charted. *Interoception,* a term used in this intervention, is defined by Fowler (2002) as "constituting the *material me* and how it relates to how we perceive feelings from our bodies that determine our mood, sense of well-being and emotions" (p. 1505). When a person has experienced trauma, they have essentially lost power over the self. Encouraging interoception invites the client to notice the present physical experience and to intentionally shift the experience.

Step-by-Step Instructions

1. Invite the client to draw a form of a person on paper or whiteboard. This can be a stick person, or three stacked circles, similar to a snowman.
2. Invite the client to pay attention to what is felt on their body in this moment. This is called *interoception* and is a very useful mindfulness skill. If the client needs help, invite noticing where the seat touches the chair, or the foot touches the floor, or hand touches the table or desk.
3. Invite the client to use different marks, hashes, lines, or shapes to represent different pressure points. Encourage the client to identify subtle differences, such as the difference in the feel of the shirt on the shoulders compared to the foot on the ground, and to represent these differences with lines and shapes. Continue encouraging the client to notice more, maybe by pointing out subtle differences if weight is shifted or focus is drawn to another point on the body.
4. Reflect on this activity with the client. Encourage the client to notice how difficult it may be to notice the body at first, but that it becomes easier and faster as the activity continues.
5. Ask the client if they used any particular strategy to find pressure points and how they decided on different shapes.
6. Invite the client to draw another body form on a second piece of paper.
7. Discuss the physical, emotional, and cognitive influence of danger and safety needs on the brain and how that might influence the body (see Know Your Brain, page 101).
8. Invite the client to consider common physical responses, such as tingling of the hair on the neck or increased heart rate. You might offer a thought experiment for the client to imagine, such as hearing the fire alarm but not necessarily sensing smoke or fire, and what might happen in the body.

Figure 4.4 In the figure on the left, safety messaging in the body; the figure on the right shows normal bodily awareness and sensory perception.

9. Invite the client to complete the new body form, this time imagining the influence of safety needs on the body. Stay attuned to the needs of the client during this activity and offer grounding through presence, conversation, or participation as needed.
10. Reflect on this activity with the client, and what it was like to shift into the mind state of danger and safety needs. Acknowledge the power of the memory and the swift action of fear on the mind and body, and perhaps acknowledge anything you notice in your own body when you think about danger and safety needs.
11. Finally, offer the third piece of paper to the client and invite the client to, once again, practice interoception and return the focus to pressure points on the body.
12. Discuss with the client the practice of shifting between states again. If desired, align the three images to discuss the differences and similarities. Invite the client to reflect on the challenges of shifting between the three different activities and anything they notice, either about the images or about the practice.
13. Acknowledge the client's effort in participating in the activity, as shifting bodily awareness is quite challenging but becomes easier with practice. Discuss the practice of grounding in the body when danger and safety signals arise in the body. Acknowledge the client's awareness of where their safety signals are in the body, and the ability to shift and ground in the present through bodily awareness.
14. Invite the client to notice their body as they are leaving the session and heading toward their next destination, particularly as they sit down in another location.

Guiding Questions

- When is it easy to bring awareness to the body?
- What are some distractions to body awareness?
- What are the challenges of nonjudgmental body awareness? Do you notice an impulse to shift your awareness to something else?
- Do any emotions arise when you notice these places in your personal space (for example, neck pain being equated with stress)?
- How do you think that body awareness in the present connects to our discussions about safety?
- What are the challenges to returning to awareness of the body?

Tips/Ways to Change

- Sensitivity to the client's needs for privacy and safety when introducing this activity is critical. If the client has experienced a physical trauma, such as sexual violence, or has an injury or disability, this activity may not be well-suited.
- Sometimes inviting clients to participate in any kind of art-making results in self-criticism and hesitancy. I find that participating with the client and showing my stick-figure drawing skills helps with this and brings a little humor to the activity.
- Resist the desire to make meaning of what the client notices, but instead just notice without judgment.
- You can find body outlines on various websites online to print.
- Often when clients experience fear, other symptoms arise, such as anger or anxiety. If appropriate for the client, introduce a second body form of the anger or anxiety, and invite the client to explore how the fear/safety body form relates to the anger/anxiety body form. Discussion could include the protective nature of anger and how different emotions work together to help us feel safe, with a focus toward improved management of the relationship with and between these emotion states.
- This activity pairs well with Shield/Wand (page 107), where work with the client includes developing a safety metaphor, possibly deciding when the shield is helpful and when it is a burden.

NOTES

ATTUNING TO THE SAFETY OF OTHERS

AMOUNT OF TIME

5–10 minutes

MATERIALS NEEDED

- Access to a window
- Various movie or video clips (optional)

Type of Activity

Relational

Intent/Used for . . .

This activity allows the client to focus on body awareness, recognizing the influence of external factors and people on their own bodies. The intervention also introduces a grounding strategy that uses a 'calm other' to reduce arousal.

Step-by-Step Instructions

1. Discuss the quick response of the body and mind when we experience a lack of safety or a sense of danger. Invite the client to express some of the things that they notice in the body when there is a sense of danger or alarm (see Ug the Caveman, page 7 for a list of physiological responses).
2. Discuss the quick response of the body and mind when there is a sense of excitement or readiness for something to happen. Note that some of these responses feel very similar to the sense of danger or alarm, such as moving quickly, looking around, and feeling a need to hurry.
3. Affirm the importance of this type of arousal as the body's desire to move—whether it be to run away or run toward something. A good example to offer might be waiting in line for a roller coaster or an ice cream cone, or children who cannot hold their patience and will dance around a little while waiting.
4. Discuss how our excitement or arousal is often influenced by others. Invite the client to recall an instance when being near a person led to feeding off their 'vibe' or energy, even when they did not know them.
5. Find a window with people outside, or walk outside if possible, and observe people passing. Point out the arousal level of different people outside—some might be moving very quickly, with swinging arms and high energy, while others might be sitting and observing as you are.
6. Choose a person who appears calm. This person does not need to be resting, but rather neutral. Invite the client to describe how this person appears. Invite the client to tune into the calm from the other person, very intentionally. Invite the client to mirror some of the physical evidence that the person is calm. This might mean sitting down comfortably, relaxing the face, half-smiling, or pacing the breathing to synchronize with the other person.
7. As the client attunes to this person with calmness, check your attunement to the client and your calmness as well. Reduce your physiological arousal along with the client so that if the client has a difficult time discussing, you are able to draw on your own experience.
8. Offer any changes that you note in the client—for instance, a softening of the face or change in posture. Invite the client to notice as well.
9. Reflect on the experience with the client. Remind the client of the natural desire for safety and the automatic response of the body and mind to feel overly excited when threatened.

Figure 4.5 Notice how looking at a person who appears calm and focused feels different from a person who does not.

Reflect with the client on how a calm person can reduce arousal even if they are unknown or at a distance. Highlight the physical calm that was just practiced. If appropriate, encourage the client in using this relational strategy, in addition to other strategies, toward establishing safety in the present.

Guiding Questions

- Have you ever had a 'false alarm,' where you became excited or afraid and checked in with another person?
- What did you notice when I (or the person outside or from the video) talked very fast and gestured with my arms?
- What did you notice when I (or the person being observed) slowed my voice down and was very still?
- Which of these states do you prefer?
- When do you feel safer, while in an excited state?
- When do you feel safer, while in a calm state?
- Why do you think this is an important skill to have—grounding in another person?
- Do you know anyone who might use you as a grounding presence? Why or why not?
- What if we had traveled (or looked) outside and everyone was excited and flailing, maybe running. How is this a useful signal of danger? How would this feel different if a person of authority or influence (for example, a paramedic) was present and speaking calmly?
- Sometimes people feel grounded or safe because of the actions of their pets. Sometimes people feel afraid because of the actions of their pets. Has this ever been true for you? What do you think is going on there?

Tips/Ways to Change

- This activity requires the observation of other people. If you do not have access to a window, or it is discomforting to observe people in real life, using a video clip can produce the same results and discussion.
- If the client presents other concerns related to socioemotional learning, this activity may not be suitable or effective.
- Pets provide an extraordinary grounding presence for many people who have experienced a traumatic event. Pets are often more trusted than people, as they are constant and predictable. This activity could be altered so that the person is invited to ground in an animal—it could be their pet, images of animals, or a video of an animal. You can take this further by exploring safety/alarm animals as a metaphor and an additional tool toward exploring safety in attuning to others.
- If the client is having difficulties recalling an incident of being affected by another person's energy, showing a video of a giggling child will almost always elicit a response. There are also wonderful videos of laughter yoga available online that exemplify attuning to others.
- When noting the effects of others on our minds and bodies, feel free to use yourself as an example. What would it be like for the client if suddenly you became very excited, stood up, and waved your arms? Would they notice an increase in heart rate, or maybe some new and confused thoughts?
- As a possible homework, consider these activities: invite the client to notice one calm person in their daily travels today, or invite the client to *be* one calm person in their daily travels today.

NOTES

▶ SELF-GRATITUDE BRAINSTORM

Type of Activity

Group

AMOUNT OF TIME

15–30 minutes

Intent/Used for . . .

This group activity highlights resilience, strength, and usefulness of the physical body. As a group, the participants reflect together on ways their body has served and protected them, with a focus toward acknowledgment and self-gratitude.

MATERIALS NEEDED

- Butcher or craft paper
- Tape
- Colored pencils or markers
- Note paper (optional)
- Envelopes (optional)
- Pens (optional)

Step-by-Step Instructions

1. Prior to the start of the group session, outline a body (that of a colleague works well) using a roll of butcher or craft paper. Create a full-length outline, including hands and feet if possible. Tape the outline to a wall. This positioning is preferred over a table or the floor, as it is powerful and upright, whereas lying down may seem power-over, or may recall postures where the participants did not have safety and control.
2. Invite the group to consider ways that their body has carried them through time. Consider ways that the body has provided a good and safe home. If necessary, prompt with 'just for today' and invite the participants to notice this moment, such as keeping the self balanced and upright.
3. Invite the group to consider gratitudes, or items they may be thankful for, regarding the body. Consider movement, or how the body changes food into fuel automatically.
4. Using different colored markers, write down the gratitudes within the body outline. Invite the group to call out their responses, or take turns if more appropriate.
5. As the group names different ways the body has served or protected, use alternating colors to write items inside the body, from top to bottom. If there are repeats, include the repeated items.
6. Continue prompting the group for things that they are grateful for. Perhaps as you move through the heart area on the outline, use more specific prompts, such as 'in what ways do we feel grateful for our heart?' Continue, using prompts for the belly, hands, legs, or feet as necessary.
7. After the outline is full, invite the group participants to look closely at what they have created. If it feels appropriate, slowly read through the responses from head to toe, or invite the group members to read aloud, either separately or in unison.
8. Invite the participants to write a personal note of gratitude to their own bodies to take with them.

Guiding Questions

- What is it like to consider your body in this way?
- What do you notice in your body right now, as we move through this activity?

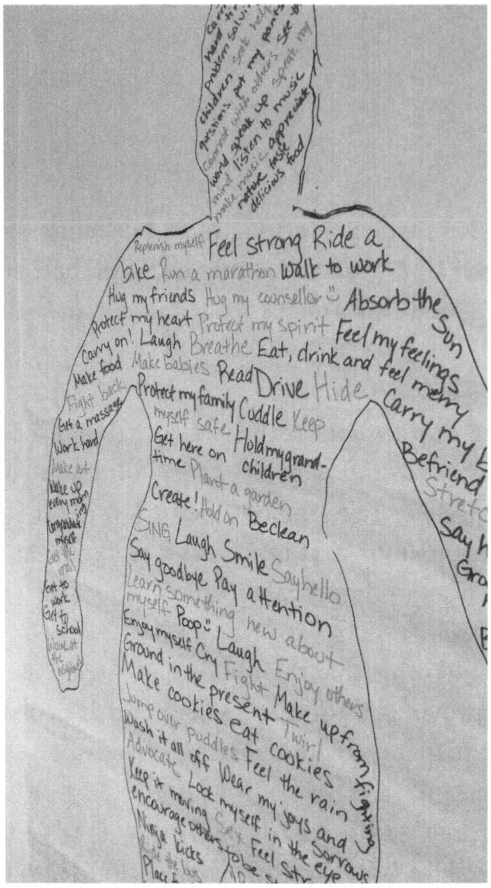

Figure 4.6 Using different colors creates a dynamic image to explore ways the body has served and protected.

- What parts of this are you hesitant to consider? When is it more difficult or troubling to consider our body in a positive or grateful way?
- How does this connect to our ongoing discussion about safety and the trauma response?

Tips/Ways to Change

- While I have seen similar activities using body forms inviting the participants to trace one another, I do not recommend this direction. I believe that this invades the personal space of the participants and may cause an emotional or physiological triggering/trauma response.
- The group participants may be offered their own colored pen and invited to take turns writing their own message inside or outside the body.
- A possible response activity may include writing around the outside of the body ways that we can get external reinforcements for these messages.

NOTES

▶ CHOICE LOG

AMOUNT OF TIME

Explanation: 10 minutes

Debrief: 15 minutes

MATERIALS NEEDED

- Paper or journal
- Pen or pencil

Type of Activity

Homework

Intent/Used for . . .

This activity emphasizes daily experiences of personal power and control. Using a daily log, clients are invited to recall events where they experienced choice and ownership over their actions and activities.

Step-by-Step Instructions

1. Invite the client to walk you through a 'typical' day in their life. Emphasize the everyday aspect of activities (for example, eating breakfast); emotionally-charged activities (for example, going to visit a child's gravesite) should be acknowledged but not dwelled upon.
2. Invite the client to consider activities they have listed, and highlight moments when the client made some sort of choice—for example, what to eat, or when to leave the house.
3. Reflect on the importance of power and control when establishing safety and reducing the trauma response. Acknowledge moments of personal choice and encourage validation of these moments of personal power. If necessary, discuss the personal power in using a grounding or safety skill to continue with daily activities rather than feeling prohibited by the trauma response.
4. Acknowledge the importance of validating these small and significant changes and how small incidents continue to grow into whole mornings or full days of personal power and choice.
5. Describe the idea of a choice log—a journal/log of every choice the client makes throughout the day. Encourage the client to share some choices that they have made already before coming to the appointment, no matter how 'small' they seem. Emphasize the choice to come to the appointment as an example of personal power over the trauma response.
6. Invite the client to maintain a choice log as homework for a specified period of time. The choice log could be kept for one day, one week, or until the next session as decided between client and counselor.

Debrief

1. Invite the client to share the experience of recording choices. In particular, allow space to unpack the ease or difficulty the task presented and if this changed throughout the duration of the homework.
2. Acknowledge the amount of choice the client has recorded in their life, and invite discussion around how these choices influence the client's life, whether they are big or small.
3. Invite the client to notice any connections between the day-to-day choices they make and their experienced sense of power or control.
4. If appropriate, encourage the client to consider choices that may feel a bit bigger in scope, but which are still within the power of the client.

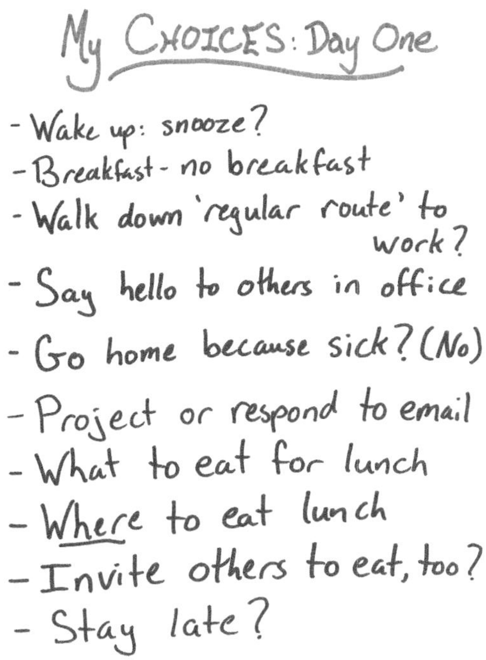

Figure 4.7 While some choices may seem trivial, recognizing one's power throughout the day is an important and healing activity.

Guiding Questions

- Take me through a typical day in your life—even the mundane things. What does it look like?
- What have you chosen to do, or not do, today—even if it seems fairly insignificant?
- When you feel like you don't have a choice, how does that impact you?

Debrief

- What have you noticed by completing this homework?
- How easy was this? Did the difficulty of the task change over time?
- Looking at some of these choices that you have made, how have they influenced you? What would have been different if you had not made those choices, or allowed somebody else to make them for you?
- How does this activity connect to some of the discussions we have had about safety, power, and control?
- What are some aspects of your life that you may have more power or control over than you realize?

Tips/Ways to Change

- Alternatively to paper and pen, electronic tools such as calendar or memo applications work well. There are a number of password-enabled journaling apps available for devices.
- If the client is currently struggling with recognizing an internal locus of control, this homework may prove difficult. The client may need additional guidance or support to complete the choice log.
- An extra challenge that can be offered is to avoid logging choices that are the same from the previous day. For example, the client does not continue to log 'what I chose for breakfast' each day, but rather a new choice that was observed.
- This is an excellent activity to complete as part of a nighttime routine.
- Some clients may benefit from expanding the choice log to include the actual decisions made as well as the choices themselves (for example, the choice is what to eat, and the decision is cereal).
- Either in preparing the client for the homework or as a debrief in the following session, introduce/emphasize the idea that not acting is still in itself a decision/choice.

NOTES

▶ OTHER RESOURCES

Cohen, B., Barnes, M., & Rankin, A. B. (1995). *Managing traumatic stress through art.* Baltimore, MD: Sidran.

Greenspan, M. (2003). *Healing through the dark emotions.* Boston, MA: Shambhala Publications.

Haskell, L. (2003). *First state trauma treatment.* Toronto, ON: Canadian Association of Mental Health.

Levine, P. (1997). *Waking the tiger.* Berkeley, CA: North Atlantic Books.

Mathieu, F. (2012). *The compassion fatigue workbook.* New York, NY: Routledge.

Moulding, N. (2016). *Gendered violence, abuse and mental health in everyday lives.* New York, NY: Routledge.

Najavits, L. M. (2001). *Seeking safety: A treatment manual for PTSD and substance abuse.* New York, NY: Routledge.

Stanley, S. (2016). *Relational and body-centered practices for healing trauma.* New York, NY: Routledge.

▶ REFERENCES

Banks, A. (2006). Relational therapy for trauma. *Journal of Trauma Practice, 5*(1), 25–47. http://dx.doi.org/10.1300/J189v05n01_03 Retrieved March 18th, 2016.

Blaustein, M. & Kinniburgh, K. (2010). *Treating traumatic stress in children and adolescents.* New York, NY: Guilford.

Bouson, J. B. (2010). *Embodied shame: Uncovering female shame in contemporary women's writings.* New York, NY: SUNY.

Complex Trauma Task Force. (2012). *The ISTSS expert consensus treatment guidelines for complex PTSD in adults.* Terrace, IL: International Society for Traumatic Stress Studies.

Courtois, C. & Ford, J. (2013). *Treatment of complex trauma: A sequenced, relationship-based approach.* New York, NY: Guilford.

Cusack, K., Jonas, D. E., Forneris, C. A., Windes, C., Sonis, J., Cook Middleton, J., Feltner, C., Brownley, K. A., Olmsted, K. R., Greenblatt, A., Weil, A., & Gaynes, B. N. (2016). Psychological treatments for adults with posttraumatic stress disorder: A systematic review and meta-analysis. *Clinical Psychology Review, 43,* 128–141. http://dx.doi.org/10.1016/j.cpr.2015.10.003 Retrieved March 18th, 2016.

Duran, E. (2006). *Healing the soul wound.* New York, NY: Teachers College Press.

Emerson, D. (2015). *Trauma-sensitive yoga in therapy.* New York, NY: Norton & Co.

Emerson, D. & Hopper, E. (2011). *Overcoming trauma through yoga.* Berkeley, CA: North Atlantic Books.

Family & Youth Services Bureau. (n.d.). Calm through creativity: How arts can aid trauma recovery. *National Clearinghouse on Families and Youth.* Retrieved February 17th, 2016 from http://ncfy.acf.hhs.gov/

Ford, J. D. & Blaustein, M. E. (2013). Systemic self-regulation: A framework for trauma-informed services in residential juvenile justice programs. *Journal of Family Violence, 28*(7), 665–677. http://dx.doi.org/10.1007/s10896-013-9538-5 Retrieved March 18th, 2016.

Fowler, C. (2002). Review of the book *Visceral Sensory Neuroscience: Interoception. Brain, 126*(6), 1505–1506. http://dx.doi.org/10.1093/brain/awg120 Retrieved March 18th, 2016.

Graham, L. (2013). *Bouncing back.* Novato, CA: New World Library.

Hass-Cohen, N. & Findlay, J. (2009). Pain, attachment, and meaning making: Report on art therapy relational neuroscience assessment protocol. *Arts in Psychotherapy, 36,* 175–184. http://dx.doi.org/10.1016/j.aip.2009.02.003 Retrieved March 18th, 2016.

Heinstein, E., Wolin, J., & Rose, S. (2014). *Trauma informed community building.* San Francisco, CA: Bridge Housing Corporation.

Herman, J. (1992). *Trauma and recovery.* New York, NY: Harper Collins.

King, M. L. (1963). *Letter from the Birmingham Jail.* Retrieved February 3rd, 2016 from https://www.africa.upenn.edu/Articles_Gen/Letter_Birmingham.html

Kinniburgh, K. & Blaustein, M. (2005). *Attachment, self-regulation and competency: A framework for intervention with traumatized youth.* National Child Traumatic Stress Network. Retrieved February 1st, 2016 from www.nctsn.org

Lasseter, J. (Producer), Docter, P., & del Carmen, R. (Directors). (2015). *Inside out* [Motion Picture]. Emeryville, CA: Pixar.

Lusebrink, N. (2004). Art therapy and the brain: An attempt to understand the underlying processes of art expression in therapy. *Art Therapy, 21*(3), 125–135. http://dx.doi.org/10.1080/07421656.2004.10129496 Retrieved March 18th, 2016.

National Institute of Mental Health. (2016). *Coping with traumatic events.* Retrieved February 1st, 2016 from http://www.nimh.nih.gov/health/topics/coping-with-traumatic-events/

Nilamadhab, K. (2011). Cognitive behavioral therapy for the treatment of post-traumatic stress disorder: A review. *Journal of Neuropsychiatric Disease and Treatment, 7,* 167–181. http://dx.doi.org/10.2147/NDT.S10389 Retrieved March 18th, 2016.

Ogden, P., Minton, K., & Pain, C. L. (2006). *Trauma and the body: A sensorimotor approach to psychotherapy.* New York, NY: Norton & Co.

Qi, W., Gevonden, M., & Shalev, A. (2016). Prevention of post-traumatic stress disorder after trauma: Current evidence and future directions. *Anxiety Disorders, 23,* 18–20. http://dx.doi.org/10.1007/s11920-015-0655-0 Retrieved March 18th, 2016.

Rothschild, B. (2000). *The body remembers: The psychophysiology of trauma and trauma treatment.* New York, NY: Norton & Co.

Rowe, M. (2016). How evidence-based is your trauma treatment? *American Psychological Association.* Retrieved February 17th, 2016 from www.apa.org

US Department of Veterans Affairs. (2015). *National Center for PTSD: Overview of psychotherapy for PTSD.* Retrieved from http://www.ptsd.va.gov/professional/treatment/overview/overview-treatment-research.asp

van der Kolk, B. (2006). Clinical implications of neuroscience research in PTSD. *Annals of the New York Academy of Sciences, 1071,* 1–17. http://dx.doi.org/10.1196/annals.1364.022 Retrieved March 18th, 2016.

Van Dernoot Lipsky, L. (2009). *Trauma stewardship.* San Francisco, CA: Berrett-Koehler.

Weinstein, E., Wolin, J., & Rose, S. (2014). *Trauma informed community building: A model for strengthening community in trauma affected neighborhoods.* San Francisco, CA: Bridge Housing Corporation.

5 Relationships and Communication

▶ WHAT ARE *RELATIONSHIP AND COMMUNICATION* CONCERNS?

Relational dynamics and styles of attachment have been explored by a number of theorists as a way of explaining expectations in relationships. Theories of relationships have also been used to explore styles of approach, communication, and avoidance. These relational and attachment theories often attribute communication patterns to early relationships, such as those from childhood and adolescence; continued socioemotional growth through participation in interpersonal interactions and community belonging also serve to enhance and change how people communicate and relate with each other. Relationship and communication concerns typically arise when expectations and needs within a relationship are unclear, when previous experience influences current relationships in a disruptive way, or when there is simply a gap in the skillset needed to identify needs within relationships. When working with clients, this phrase, and others noted throughout the chapter, may be indicators that they are having difficulties in communicating or relating to others.

"You can't trust anyone in this world."

As relational interactions shape us across the lifespan, how relationships are ultimately enacted is something that is learned through time and experiences, both of which can be pleasant or unpleasant. We enter into relationships using tools, styles, and approaches based on things we have learned from previous relationships. Life experiences that include relational betrayals or breaches of trust can result in a broad, and sometimes universal, *distrust*. While this can be a form of self-protection, and therefore a useful form of coping, it can also result in isolation and loneliness.

"I tell everyone everything."

At the opposing extreme of communication, those who have struggled in gaining acknowledgment or validation, or who have experienced little positive reinforcement, may have a tendency to *over share*. Aggressively seeking relationships, or being too open with communication, can prove distancing in relationships, whether this is with partners, friends, or colleagues. Finding a balance of how and when to disclose thoughts and feelings is an important communication and relationship skill.

"I've lost myself."

Self-location—identifying what we feel and desire, and how to communicate those needs—is a critical concern in developing and maintaining healthy relationships. This is explored in some detail in the Identity chapter (page 157); however, who we are and how we want to be present in the world affects how we present ourselves to others. At times we learn about our identity primarily through various reflections on the self in social interactions. During adolescence, for instance, youth adopt characteristics of the peer group (Siegel, 2013). When beginning new romantic relationships, partners may develop or assimilate some of the values or characteristics of the other partner (Carbonneau, Vallerand, Lavigne, & Paquet, 2016). This flexibility with self-hood offers options for 'trying on' new aspects of the self. However, aligning with the values of another for the benefit of the relationship may result in self-confusion. Further, feeling 'lost' in a relationship does not improve the relationship itself, but rather strains the membership and increases the risk of disconnection (Firestone, 2009).

"Every counselor I have ever had is the same."

The *therapeutic alliance*—that is, the relationship and communication between client and counselor, and the ability to collaborate with the client toward client-oriented needs—remains the most predictive factor in whether a person stays in therapy and whether a client notices any beneficial change (Duncan, Miller, Wampold, & Hubble, 1999). Most readers will be familiar with the stereotype of a counselor: a Freud-type individual looking over a notepad while the client sits in a low chair or sofa and answers probing questions about childhood. This image and the history behind it represents a metaphor of power-over, with the counselor appearing all-knowing and the client in a rather child-like position (see Siegel, 2010).

On the other hand, good clinical practice includes getting to know the client as a whole person, and allowing the client to practice power and safety in the relationship. Communication exchanges between the counselor and client should reflect this process. This might include evaluating the different preferred styles of counselor-client interaction, knowing how and when to share collaborative feedback, and exploring how these communication activities might be useful in relationships outside of the counseling setting.

▶ RELEVANCE

As relationship and communication define a therapeutic alliance, it is safe to presume that these are *primary* concerns of moving forward with all therapeutic collaboration. Research from the International Center for Clinical Excellence estimated a 50% drop-out rate for clients who do not feel a collaborative relationship with the helping professional (Miller, 2015). Given this statistic, relationship and communication concerns are relevant to every client, in addition to any other presenting therapeutic goals or clinical concerns.

Within and beyond the counseling setting, relationships defined by safety, accountability, and cooperation are protective against a number of clinical concerns. Healthy relationships also prove to be protective in the case of experiencing adverse events, such as natural disasters or trauma. Research indicates that the presence of supportive relationships predicts a more effective resolution to clinical issues, such as depression (Feeney & Collins, 2014). Conversely, relationships that include intimidation, inequity, blaming, or minimizing lead to unhealthy relational patterns that are disruptive at best, and at the extreme may constitute abuse (Velonis, 2016). Relationship and communication skills have also been identified as critical to socioemotional learning across the lifespan. Reflecting on hopes for future relationships, and how historical relationships influence communication styles, offers a coherent life narrative and a sense of personal continuity (Arbeit, Hershberg, Rubin, DeSouza, & Lerner, 2016; Marraffa & Paternoster, 2016).

Many readers will have participated in a less-than-desirable relationship at some point and might have recognized the difficulties but hesitated in making a change. Communicating needs and limits in a relationship, as well as creating and managing new relationships and endings, are common human challenges. Some relationship concerns are relatively straightforward and readily transformed with communication skills practice. Others may present as pathology, such as avoidance, loneliness, depression, or risk-taking, as well as conduct concerns such as substance misuse or oppositional behaviors. A discussion exploring relationships underlying these pathologies may highlight some relational desires that are well-suited to interventions outlined in this chapter.

▶ WHAT WORKS WELL

Effective communication skills prove potent in easing some relational concerns. Effective communication is essentially listening with clarification and reflection, including awareness of cognitions and the effect of self and others. This includes not only verbal but body language, tone, and attention. Beyond listening and sharing information, respectful communication includes trust, safety, cooperation, and accountability.

One way in which a client can build both communication and relationship skills is through self-location. This practice invites mindfulness of personal needs, as well as how those needs influence what is shared and what is heard. Acknowledging personal emotions, needs, and cognitions allows the communicator to identify intentions within the interaction, and further, within the relationship. Across relationships, an individual is often aided by identifying their hopes and needs from the other.

Relationship-specific therapies, such as family and couples counseling, focus on understanding development needs and style differences in communication. Conflict resolution skills, including de-escalation of strong emotions and collaborative problem-solving, are common elements of relationship counseling. While this book does not cover couples-based interventions, identifying strengths in the individual and increasing positive interactions in relationships are common goals in counseling for families and couples, and therefore many of the following interventions can be adapted appropriately.

Perhaps the most well-known theorists within relationship counseling are John and Julie Gottman. The Drs. Gottman defined the Four Horsemen of relationships, communicative elements that predict relational discord. Criticism, defensiveness, 'stonewalling,' and contempt have been identified in their research as consistent negative mindsets that result in ending relationships. Interventions to reduce these negative interactions resulted in the Sound Relationship House; this 'house' includes understanding life dreams of the self and other. Encouraging aspirations of each other, and finding daily opportunities to express fondness, admiration, and appreciation, result in personal and relational growth. Gottman and Gottman based their research and intervention strategies on over 40 years of longitudinal research. This work is now considered foundational for relationship and communication counseling (Gottman & Krokoff, 1989; Gurman, Lebo, & Snyder, 2015).

The Duluth Model of relationships and communication (Pence & Paymar, 1993) uses the Power and Control Wheel to offer skills and education for those using abusive or oppressive communication in relationships. The Duluth Model includes awareness education on resisting using behaviors that are coercive, intimidating, isolating, and abusive, all of which are hallmarks of unhealthy relationships. Operationalizing respectful communication, including negotiation, shared responsibility, honesty, and non-threatening behavior, provide a starting point for skill-building and conflict resolution in this model.

Common themes across relationship and communication interventions include clear expression of wants and needs, evaluating and balancing the needs of the other in the relationship, and further, understanding personal ideas about the self and self-in-relationship.

▶ FUTURE RESEARCH

The relationship and communication styles and dynamics of adolescence remain a topic of interest in emerging research. Adolescence, marked by physiological and emotional zest, includes the ever-changing social environment of school, where youth are faced with a number of different communication styles and a breadth of relationships unlike any other life period. These predictable, but meaningful, shifts in relationships, attachments, and power dynamics, influence communicative behaviors and identification with social groups. These changes also influence emotion and mood states, where researchers continue to connect experiences of perceived popularity, loneliness, and social anxiety to the interactions between adolescent development and environmental changes and responses (Al-Yagon, Kopelman-Rubin, Brunstein, & Mikulincer, 2016; Cavanaugh & Buehler, 2016; Su, Pettit, & Erath, 2016).

Notably, this area of research is also growing with the elder age group, as the aging population relocates to new homes and new social networks. These changes are also occurring for the aging alongside a number of physiological and emotional changes, similar to those during adolescence (Kojola & Moen, 2016; Liao & Brunner, 2016).

The heightened influence of technology is also relevant to exploring relationships and communication. Some researchers point to an increased use of technology as influencing the sense of connection and the ability to share thoughts and feelings within the safety of a distant relationship—with both positive and negative outcomes (Kim, LaRose, & Peng, 2009; Ryan & Xenos, 2011). Others tend toward the use of technology to retain a feeling of romantic or family connection for those distanced or away, such as deployed military or disaster relief workers (Carter & Renshaw, 2016; Madianou, 2016). Gaming is also emerging as a technology-based relationship, with research exploring learned communication amidst other socioemotional barriers, such as Autism Spectrum Disorder (Fein, 2015; Martoncik & Loksa, 2016).

▶ INTERVENTIONS IN THIS CHAPTER

Psychoeducational

Four Components of Awkward Conversations (page 133): This intervention gives the client information that can help in navigating tricky conversations with loved ones, friends, or colleagues.

Talk-Based/Motivational

The Ideal You (page 136): Using future-driven thought, this intervention allows the client to focus on themselves within various relationships and how their actions can influence others' perceptions.

Art-Based

Mirror Drawing (page 139): This intervention invites the client to practice relational attunement, including pacing, and explores physical space in relationships.

Hands-On

Balancing (page 142): A variation on traditional trust-based activities, this intervention highlights the importance of considering all people involved in a relationship.

Relational

The Novel You (page 145): This activity invites experimenting with perspective-taking, and also involves an exploration of important relationships in the life of the client.

Group

Relationship Paradoxes (page 148): In this intervention, drawing on the notion of paradoxical traits, group members are encouraged to consider contrary aspects of their current self in relation to others.

Homework

Role-Modeling Communication (page 151): Through the use of 'I statements,' this homework invites clients to become a role model of healthy communication when interacting with others in their lives.

▶ FOUR COMPONENTS OF AWKWARD CONVERSATIONS

AMOUNT OF TIME

10–15 minutes

MATERIALS NEEDED

- Paper (optional)
- Pen (optional)

Type of Activity

Psychoeducational

Intent/Used for . . .

This intervention is intended to give the client background information and education on introducing awkward conversations. Awkwardness can be experienced when bringing up sensitive topics with loved ones, though the information in this intervention can be used in a variety of conversational situations. It is particularly useful when a client is having difficulty opening up to somebody in their life about a specific topic, despite knowing that the conversation could be considered necessary or healthy.

Step-by-Step Instructions

1. Invite the client to consider awkward conversations that they have had in the past. The client does not need to share intimate details; however, they should brainstorm general topics and situations that create a sensation of 'awkwardness.'
2. Introduce the idea that everybody feels awkward at certain points in their lives; for some people, awkward conversations are few and far between, whereas for others they seem to be a daily occurrence.

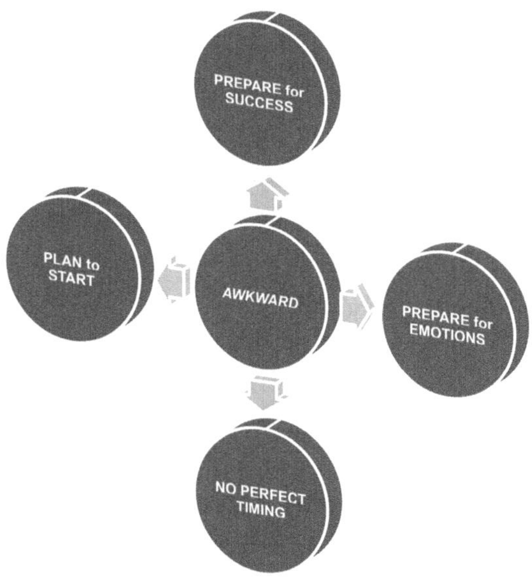

Figure 5.1 It is important to note that a life spent avoiding awkwardness would be quite boring.

3. Let the client know that because of this, there are some tips that have come out of both psychology and peoples' experiences, all of which can sometimes help when bringing up awkward topics of conversation/discussion.
4. The first tip is to set oneself up for success. This means setting goals for the conversation, as well as recognizing and planning for behavioral patterns (such as interrupting, avoiding, etc.) that have been barriers to similar conversations in the past.
5. The second tip is to recognize that awkwardness inevitably leads to emotions—the client should not expect to experience calm during an awkward conversation and therefore could benefit from identifying (and planning for) what emotions may arise. Identifying possible emotions for both themselves as well as their conversational partner is important.
6. The third tip is to recognize that there is never a perfect time for opening up an awkward conversation. Often, clients will avoid or put off conversations altogether with the justification that the 'time wasn't right.' Despite this, note that it may be prudent to still invite the client to consider what times or locations may offer the best opportunities to hold a conversation, even knowing that the ideal situation may not ever arise.
7. Finally, it is important for the client to spend some time thinking about their first two sentences—how would they like to open the conversation? More often than not, it is the beginning of a conversation that feels awkward; once the conversation has begun, the awkwardness tends to disappear fairly quickly.
8. Summarize the four tips and note how they may apply to the client's situation. Invite the client to identify a specific conversation they have been avoiding, and using this as an example, develop a possible plan for addressing the awkwardness.

Guiding Questions

- Tell me about some times when you felt a conversation was awkward.
- What, for you, made those situations awkward? Are there any themes to the situations or topics?
- Thinking back to other awkward conversations, are there things that you or your partner/friend/other do that may prevent a conversation from happening?
- What emotions do you think you might start to feel when bringing up this topic?
- In your mind, what would be the 'perfect' time to bring this up? Why? What if that time/situation never arises?
- How would you like the first few things that you say to sound? What actual words will you use?

Tips/Ways to Change

- Depending on the time available, it is often useful to go more in-depth for each of the four tips and invite the client to strategize for their situation. For example, in the first step, encourage the client to develop their own goals for the intended awkward conversation.
- Adding a practice component after going through the four tips is a great way to help the client gain confidence before actually entering into the real-life situation.
- Alternatively, for homework, the client can jot down initial thoughts or goals for the conversation.

NOTES

▶ THE IDEAL YOU

AMOUNT OF TIME

- 20 minutes

MATERIALS NEEDED

- Paper (optional)
- Pen (optional)

Type of Activity

Talk-based/Motivational

Intent/Used for . . .

This activity is designed to allow clients to see where they may have some control and/or power in how they shape their lives. Because of this, it is great for clients who are struggling with identity and relationship issues in the present, or those whose external circumstances are creating a lower sense of self-worth.

Step-by-Step Instructions

1. Begin by inviting the client to picture themselves 10 years from now. Emphasize that 10 years is not a very long time, but it is also not tomorrow, so some things are likely to have changed.
2. Ask the client to list off qualities that, in 10 years, they would like their partner (and/or friends, co-workers, etc.) to use to describe the client. For example, how would they like their partner/friends to complete the sentence "My partner is so . . ."
3. For each quality, invite the client to then describe what it is they will be doing in 10 years that will lead their partner/friends/etc. to say such things. The focus of this step is to allow the client to consider behaviors and actions, rather than ideals. Encourage the client to consider more general behaviors, rather than spending too much time focusing on specific details of the future that cannot be guaranteed.

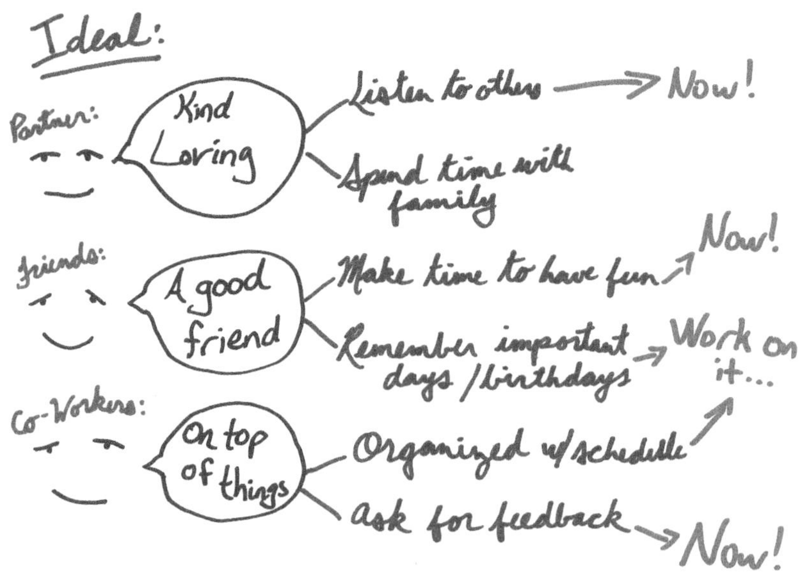

Figure 5.2 Identifying future goals is one way to enhance current relationships.

4. Invite the client to bring some of these ideas back into the present and to identify current behaviors or actions that may be in line with what they are planning to do or exemplify in 10 years.
5. Encourage the client to frame their current behaviors and attitudes in the context of setting themselves up for success in the future.

Guiding Questions

- Would it be all right to try a thought experiment?
- In 10 years, what types of things would you like your partner (friends, co-workers) to be saying about you? What types of adjectives do you hope they would use to describe you?
- How will that feel, when people are saying those things about you?
- What types of things would you be doing 10 years from now that would cause people to say these things, or to describe you in that way?
- Are you doing any of those things now?
- I wonder what it would be like to think about having those qualities now, not just in 10 years.
- Can you give me an example?
- What could you do over the next few weeks that may help you to get a start on some of these things?

Tips/Ways to Change

- Be sure to continue summarizing and emphasizing the qualities the client is listing throughout this activity.
- When discussing current behaviors, encourage the client to give both specific and general examples.
- It is also possible to expand upon how the client will be *feeling* in 10 years when their partner/friends/etc. will be saying these things.
- This is an excellent intervention to lead into homework. Possible homework can include: picking one desired quality to focus on, considering behaviors as a whole, or expanding more upon the 'future self' story.

NOTES

▶ MIRROR DRAWING

Type of Activity

Art-based

AMOUNT OF TIME

5–10 minutes

MATERIALS NEEDED

- Paper
- Pen or pencil
- Crayons (optional)

Intent/Used for . . .

This activity aims to practice relational attunement, including pacing, and exploring physical space in relationships. The focus on attunement can be a useful and thought-provoking experience for clients who are struggling with connecting to or with others. While the activity invites discussion around a metaphor, the embodiment of the activity can be used as an intervention on its own, even without discussion.

Step-by-Step Instructions

1. Fold a piece of paper in half, and then unfold it. Note the crease; drawing a line across the crease is optional.
2. Offer the client a pen, or crayon if preferred. Share with the client that this partner activity will be completed in-session.
3. Describe the activity briefly: you will be creating a shared image by drawing at the same time on a single piece of paper; the counselor will start.
4. Place your pen on the center crease and invite the client to do the same, positioning opposite, as if looking in a mirror. Instruct the client to follow your movement. As a warmup, slowly draw the line toward your body and instruct the client to move their pen toward their body, as though looking in a mirror.

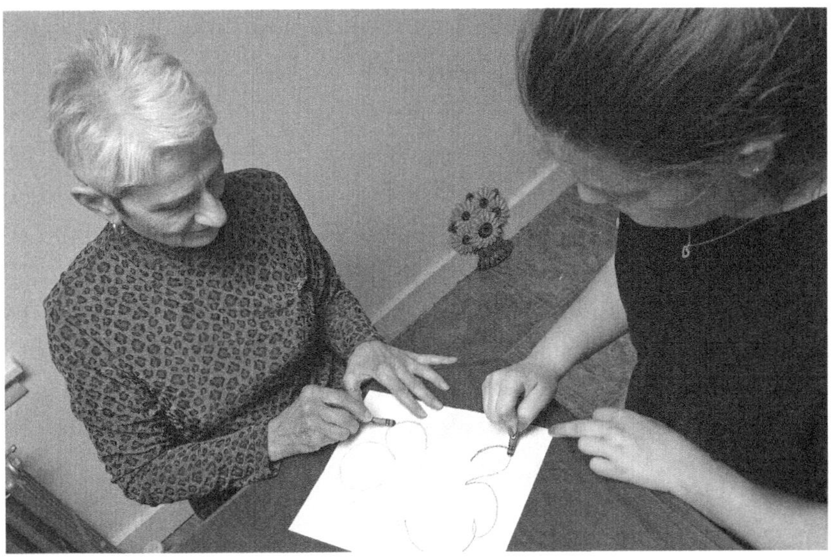

Figure 5.3 While difficult, matching the pace of another is an important aspect of relationships and communication.

5. Continue, using a very slow pace. Attune to the client. Invite the client to continue following the line drawing, and perhaps make a simple shape like a square so that the client may reasonably predict what will be made.
6. Begin to draw more challenging lines or shapes, such as a circle, or a number of wavy lines. The goal is not to attempt to create an image, but rather to invite the client to attune to the pace of the therapist.
7. Invite the client to voice needs, if slowing down or speeding up is desired.
8. Invite the client to take the lead, and follow the client. Use gentle language to slow the pace down if necessary. Further, if the client is interested in starting with a clean sheet of paper, offer the option.
9. Laughter is recommended.
10. Explore the shared experience of this exercise. Invite the client to reflect on preferring to lead or follow. Share any observations of pace, energy, and attunement.
11. Connect this exercise with enacting relationship. Invite reflection on whether the actions in the activity align with the client's experience in relationships.

Guiding Questions

- What were your expectations at the start of this activity?
- Did you prefer leading or following?
- Did you notice if you were tense or relaxed physically during the activity? Did one state or the other help you to participate?
- Did you find yourself trying to anticipate my movements?
- Did you find yourself becoming frustrated when I could not anticipate *your* movements?
- What do you notice about yourself in this activity? Are any of these things also fitting for your communication or relationship style?
- What would have made this easier? What made it easy? Do any of these things fit for your communication or relationship style?
- What made this difficult? What would have made it more difficult? Do any of these things fit for your communication or relationship style?

Tips/Ways to Change

- I prefer legal size paper, but any size will work.
- This activity can be altered to be a mirror movement activity, although care should be taken if the client is sensitive to physical closeness.
- If appropriate for the client, invite the client to fill in the lines with abstract colors, or to find images to fill them in.
- This activity works well with finger paints and can expand the embodied and sensory experience. Using a large piece of craft or media paper, spill a puddle of finger paint across the center line. Mirroring, drag the hand or fingers through the paint to a shared image.

NOTES

▶ BALANCING

AMOUNT OF TIME

5 minutes

MATERIALS NEEDED

- Long towel, such as a beach towel

Type of Activity

Hands-on

Intent/Used for . . .

This activity encourages immediate, in-session awareness of trust, communication, and attunement, all relevant exploration points when discussing relationship and communication concerns. This activity also includes a tense/release muscle activity, offering immediate reduction of arousal in-session. It can be particularly useful when working with those hesitant to engage in a verbal therapeutic exchange.

Step-by-Step Instructions

1. Inform the client that they are being invited to participate in an unusual balancing activity. Use humor, encouragement, and affirmation to express this sentiment.
2. Invite the client to stand in the room opposite you. Ensure the client is standing in an area where, should they lose balance, they will feel the wall behind them.
3. Using a long towel, direct the client to hold one end of the towel with two gripped hands. The helping professional will hold the other end of the towel.
4. Step backward, away from the client, to the length of the towel. Holding the towel taut, instruct the client that both client and therapist will lean back and hold each other up, balancing for a count of five.
5. Slowly, attuning to the client, lean back until you feel the client has a sense of balance. Invite the client to direct the activity, asking if you are pulling too hard or not hard

Figure 5.4 This non-verbal activity invites noticing the challenges of trust, while also providing a tense/release sensation.

enough. Invite the client to do the same, gently letting the client know your physical state.

6. Smile. Laugh. Use affirming bodily and facial expressions to model for the client how you are feeling in this activity.
7. When some sense of balance has been reached, invite the client to attempt to hold the balance for your count of five. Slowly, count down from five, maintaining the posture with the client.
8. Release and relax. Use bodily and facial expressions, and words, to describe the sensations in the body at that moment and to thank the client for keeping you balanced.
9. Invite the client to try one more time. If the client is comfortable, allow the client to direct the activity this time. This will include telling the therapist when to lean back or forward, when to provide more or less tension, and when things feel balanced. Invite the client to begin the countdown from five.
10. Release and relax. Invite the client to use words to describe sensations in the body and mind at that moment. Invite the client to express their experience during the activity.
11. Explore relationship and trust within the activity. Invite the client to discuss this balancing as a metaphor in relationships, but also how, during the activity, both participants need to use very clear language toward the objective of balancing in order to get needs met. Use your own observations to reflect what was noticed about the client, and how this might fit with a conversation about relationship and communication concerns.

Guiding Questions

- Have you done an activity like this before, maybe when you were a child?
- What did you like about this activity? When were you uncomfortable?
- Did you like leading or following? Why do you think that is? Which is easier?
- Did you have any fears? Were the fears for you or for me?
- Would you do this activity with just anyone? What type of person would you not want to do this activity with? Why?
- What do you think this has to do with relationship? Why do we practice it here?

Tips/Ways to Change

- Use care. The intention of this activity is to encourage the client toward trust and communication. It is your responsibility as the leader of this activity to ensure that the client is safe, above all things. If you are not able to balance yourself, that is okay—the important element is that the client feels balanced.
- Physical strength and some fine motor skills must be considered before attempting this activity.
- Both client and therapist should have an absence of pain or injury.
- Depending on the relative heights of the client and helping professional, you may want to do this activity from a kneeling or squatting position.
- Ensure the client is able to grip, and maintain a grip, before suggesting this activity.

NOTES

▶ THE NOVEL YOU

AMOUNT OF TIME

15–20 minutes

MATERIALS NEEDED

- Sticky notes
- Pen or pencil
- Whiteboard (optional)
- Dry-erase markers (optional)

Type of Activity

Relational

Intent/Used for . . .

This activity invites experimenting with perspective-taking, and also involves exploration of important relationships in the life of the client. Together, the client and helping professional discuss the bi-directional nature of relationships, the client's strengths in relationship, and shifting relational perspective between self and other.

Step-by-Step Instructions

1. Invite the client to name four persons playing an important role in the client's life. These individuals should be ones with whom the client has interacted, persons that would have experienced the client inter personally. Invite the client to write the names of these four individuals on sticky notes.
2. Using a wall, table, or other space where you can spread out, invite the client to situate these sticky notes at some distance from each other.
3. Invite the client to choose one of the individuals. Invite the client to name three things that this individual would say about the client. Encourage the client to consider self-characteristics, considering interpersonal interactions that would influence what the person knows or perceives about the client.
4. Invite the client to write short descriptions of named characteristics on sticky notes and situate these around the named relationship.

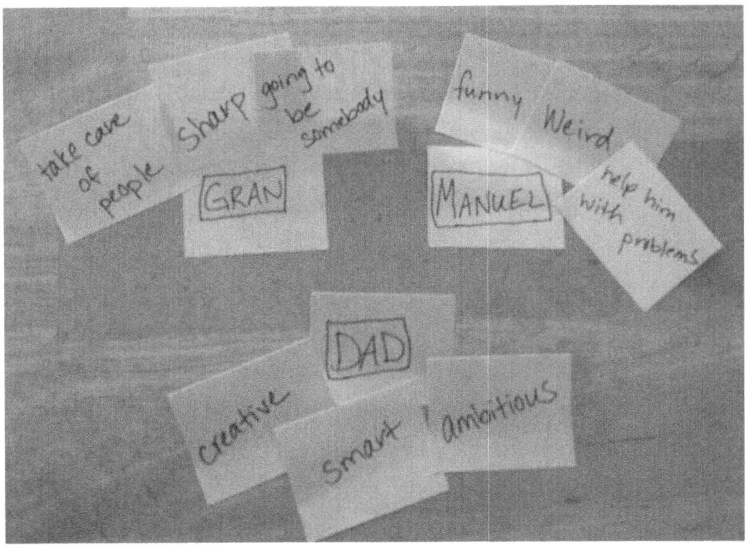

Figure 5.5 Which of these characteristics feels the most natural? Where are you comfortable enacting the relationship?

5. Continue with the other three individuals. If time allows, allow the client to story particular instances or circumstances that provide evidence to these client characteristics. You may also share your observations of characteristics of the client that emerge within these storied circumstances.
6. After completion, invite the client to review what has been written and to reflect on these characteristics. If the client notices something is missing, invite the client to add a few more, if desired.
7. Discuss how personal characteristics, how we perceive ourselves, and how we perceive how others see us, influence our way of enacting relationship. If appropriate, invite the client to explore ways that they enact a relationship differently with one character than with another, and yet they continue to be the same whole person. This complex idea invites discussion about how a client may shift how they are in relationships and identify skills that work with one relationship that may also work with another.

Guiding Questions

- Which one of these character descriptions feels most comfortable? Least comfortable?
- Which one of these character descriptions do you like the most? Why?
- Which one of these character descriptions is the most challenging for you to maintain?
- Are there any of these descriptions that you wish were not true?
- In these relationships, is there one more thing that you would like this person to say about you, but that they might not know about you yet?
- Which of these individuals brings out the best in you? Why?
- Why do you think we do this activity? How might this be helpful to the work that we are doing together?

Tips/Ways to Change

- The named individuals do not necessarily need to be individuals who know the client well, if the client has difficulty naming four.
- A smaller or larger number of relationships can be named as time and necessity allow.
- This activity does not have to include relationships that are deep or meaningful. Rather, any relationship can be explored, such as the interaction with the store clerk, doctor, or teacher. 'Counselor' can also be an incredibly interesting relationship to explore perspective-taking, and to invite the client to fully collaborate in the process of counseling.
- While the description here highlights enacting relationships, this activity can also focus more toward empathy and perspective-taking. A powerful take-home activity includes inviting the client to choose one individual and, through the perceived voice of that individual, the client writes a letter to self from that individual.
- Invite the client to imagine using relationship characteristics from one relationship in another. Discuss how this flexibility helps the client get what is needed from the relationship.
- An additional prompt through this activity may be to invite the client to imagine what this person would hope for the client through the counseling process. I find this to be useful for those who have been mandated to counseling.

NOTES

RELATIONSHIP PARADOXES

AMOUNT OF TIME

20–30 minutes

MATERIALS NEEDED

- Paper (optional)
- Markers/crayons (optional)

Type of Activity

Group

Intent/Used for . . .

Clients who are concerned about their relationships with others sometimes have a tendency to focus on one or two aspects of those relationships, and more often than not they will focus exclusively on positive traits or negative traits. This activity encourages participants in recognizing that relationships can contain paradoxical characteristics—both positive and negative at the same time. With the support of other group participants in identifying these paradoxes, clients can gain clarity in their perceptions of current relationships, in some cases sparking positive change.

Step-by-Step Instructions

1. Invite each group participant to consider one relationship in their life, noting that it can be a friend, romantic, family, or work relationship. Be sure to mention that participants will not need to share the specific relationship with the group, and the relationship does not have to be one that they have been working on previously.
2. Explain to the group that this activity will involve a bit of thought around relationships, and how sometimes our attention is drawn to only certain aspects of relationships, despite there being an element of complexity in how we interact and feel with others.
3. Invite each participant to think about an animal that best describes how they feel, think, or act in their chosen relationship.
4. One at a time, invite the group to share with each other their animal. If it is useful for participants to describe the animal for clarity, this is permitted; however, encourage the group not to dwell too long on each animal.
5. Note to the group that everybody has chosen their animal for certain reasons, not all of which will be immediately evident. Explain that many in the group likely chose the animal because of certain traits that remind them of themselves in the relationship, and that these traits sometimes take on positive or negative qualities.
6. Invite the participants to consider what some of the negative traits are that are associated with their animal. After allowing for some time to pass, invite each participant to share with the others what some of these traits may be.
7. Remind the group that our tendency in relationships is to focus on one side or the other, without always recognizing that there are both positive and negative qualities inherent in every characteristic—or, in this case, every animal.
8. Invite the participants to consider what some of the positive traits are that are associated with their animal. After allowing for some time to pass, invite each participant to share

Figure 5.6 This activity can be completed individually; however, there is strength in considering the group's perspective.

with the others what some of these traits may be. If participants are struggling, encourage other participants to suggest some positive qualities associated with the animal.

9. Explain to the group that it is important to recognize these 'paradoxical traits' within ourselves and within our relationships with others. Increasing our framework of some of our own qualities by focusing on these paradoxes can often lead to greater confidence within our relationships.
10. Invite the group to further discuss paradoxical traits in other relationships in their lives, possibly looking at relationships and dynamics within the group as well.

Guiding Questions

- Often when we talk about relationships, the focus turns to romantic relationships—what other types of relationships are there?
- When you consider a relationship that is on your mind, is it easy to see all aspects of that relationship, and your role within that relationship, immediately?
- When you think about your role within the relationship, what type of animal comes to mind? Think about the behaviors, feelings, and thoughts you experience—what animal best represents you in this relationship?
- Animals are typically not just simple and one-dimensional; sometimes they can be quite complex, though there are one or two qualities that we normally associate with specific animals. What are some of the negative characteristics people think of when they think about your animal?

- What are some of the positive characteristics people think of when they think about your animal?
- How often do you think about both sets of these characteristics? Do both sides fit with your own experience?
- What are your thoughts on paradoxical traits? Why is it useful to consider both sides of characteristics?

Tips/Ways to Change

- Animals are only one way to begin this exercise. Other options could be to associate how participants feel in relationships with careers, weather phenomenon, or specific emotions.
- Fictional animals or creatures are permitted, as well!
- Participants can also draw their animals on one side of a piece of paper, with the paradoxical traits listed on the back of the paper.
- Though much of the power of this intervention comes from the support inherent in a group setting, it can also be adapted to individual sessions led in a very similar fashion.
- Sometimes the disclosure of positive and negative traits can be quite difficult or scary, especially if clients are ashamed of their role in a relationship—depending on the group, it is also possible for each participant to share their animal, and then have the participant to their left (or right) brainstorm qualities typically associated with that animal.

NOTES

▶ ROLE-MODELING COMMUNICATION

AMOUNT OF TIME

Explanation: 20 minutes

Debrief: 15 minutes

MATERIALS NEEDED

- None

Type of Activity

Homework

Intent/Used for . . .

This activity is designed to give the client a tool ('I statements') to communicate with loved ones and other individuals in their life with whom it has been historically difficult to communicate. In particular, if the client is feeling that somebody in their life doesn't listen, role modeling 'I statements' can lead to the other person feeling respected, and ideally this activity will encourage other people in the client's life to be clearer in their own communication. Another goal of this homework is to give the client a chance to observe the effects of trying a communication style different from those that have been used up to this point in their relationship(s).

Step-by-Step Instructions

1. Explain to the client that sometimes the best way to encourage open and relevant communication is by role modeling healthy communication behavior.
2. Introduce the concept of 'I statements':
   - 'I statements' are very useful when discussions are resulting in unwanted or nonproductive arguments.
   - 'I statements' allow the communicator to introduce their thoughts without disrespecting the other person or causing the other person to feel blamed.
   - The onus when using 'I statements' is on the communicator—it is a way to take responsibility for one's emotions without minimizing the other person's impact/behavior.
3. Explain the three main components of 'I statements':
   - Identification of the triggering environmental/behavioral elements.
     For example, "When I see a coat on the floor . . ."
   - Identification of emotion being felt.
     For example, "I feel frustrated . . ."

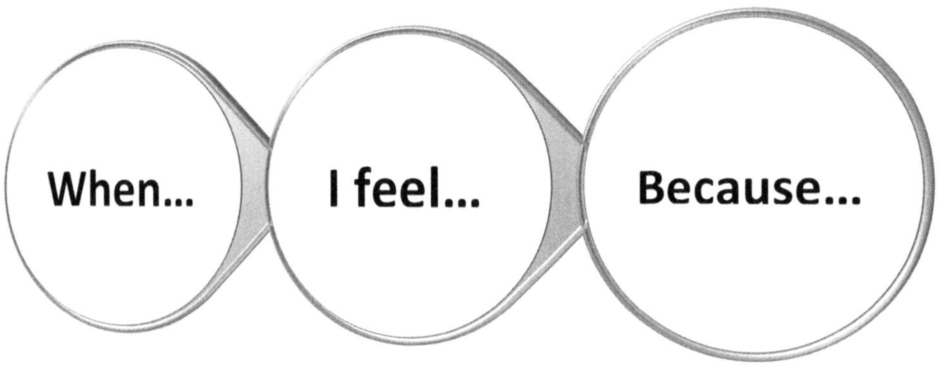

Figure 5.7 Helping professionals are also considered role models—do you use 'I statements'?

- Self-reflection/interpretation of feeling.
  For example "And I think that's because to me it's a sign that I'm being disrespected."

4. Using a few examples from the client's own experiences, invite the client to practice using 'I statements.'
5. Leave some space for questions about 'I statements' and how they can be used.
6. For homework, invite the client to:
   - Use 'I statements' any time they are having difficulty getting a message across; and
   - Note other people's reactions to the 'I statements,' including any behavior and/or communication changes.

Debrief

1. When the client returns, invite them to share their experiences of using 'I statements.'
2. Explore under what circumstances the client used 'I statements' as well as how easy or difficult this felt.
3. Invite the client to note any differences between the formal idea of 'I statements' and how they actually communicated during the homework. Normalize the concept of making 'I statements' fit for their personal communication style.
4. Discuss other people's reactions to the use of 'I statements.' Invite the client to reflect on how their role modeling can have an impact on others' behaviors and actions.

Guiding Questions

- Tell me about a time when you did not feel heard. Tell me about a time when you think you weren't hearing somebody else.
- What are some of the more common items/circumstances around which you and your (partner/family member/friend) argue?
- Tell me what, exactly, is happening—not your interpretation of it, but what you see or observe.
- How do you feel when this happens?
- I notice you've mentioned more than one emotion; tell me a bit more about each one.
- Why do you think this is?
- How do you think your (partner/family member/friend) will react when you say that? How would you *like* them to react?

Debrief

- How did using 'I statements' go for you? Tell me about when you have been using them.
- Sometimes people notice that they change the formal structure of 'I statements' to fit their own communication style better—did this happen for you? What about 'I statements' feels natural? What feels unnatural?
- What did you notice about others' reactions to 'I statements'?
- How do you think your role modeling of healthy communication can impact the people in your life?

Tips/Ways to Change

- If there is time, or if the client is coming from a rudimentary understanding of healthy communication, it may be useful before assigning this homework to educate the client on various components of communication, including verbal/nonverbal/para-verbal communication, and the role of the listener in healthy communication. If the helping professional needs refreshing, these concepts can be found and explained through a simple online search.

- When discussing the emotion identification part of 'I statements,' encourage the client to limit each statement to one emotion—if there are a number of emotions being experienced, it may require more than one 'I statement.'
- Note that 'I statements' do not need to have all three components in the exact order every time. They are the most effective when all elements are present; however, the client may prefer to reorder them, which is fine. Encourage the client to use words/phrases that work and sound best for them.
- That being said, the initial use of 'I statements' can still sound awkward for the client—use this as a chance to discuss how the client (and other people around them) may not be used to clear communication; be sure to normalize this experience. This is a great opportunity to practice and see what happens!
- If the client, during practice, is picking up the concept fairly rapidly, you may also add an experiential/drama component to it where the helping professional actually responds to what the client is saying.
- Regarding the homework itself, it can sometimes be quite daunting to think about using 'I statements' daily, so an initial homework could be to use an 'I statement' on three separate occasions before the next session—and to be prepared to discuss the situations and outcomes when they return.

NOTES

▶ OTHER RESOURCES

Brown, B. (2010). *The gifts of imperfection.* New York, NY: Gotham Books.

Duncan, B. (2014). *On becoming a better therapist.* New York, NY: American Psychiatric Association.

Gottman Institute. (2016). *Gottman Institute: A research-based approach to creating stronger relationships.* Retrieved from https://www.gottman.com/

Merrell, K. W. (2007). *Strong teens: A social and emotional learning curriculum.* Baltimore, MD: Brookes.

Mitchell, L. (2016). *Creativity as co-therapist.* New York, NY: Routledge.

Poehnell, G. & Amundson, N. E. (2011). *Hope-filled engagement.* Richmond, BC: Ergon.

▶ REFERENCES

Al-Yagon, M., Kopelman-Rubin, D., Brunstein, A., & Mikulincer, M. (2016). Four-model approach to adolescent-parent attachment relationships and adolescents loneliness, school belonging, and teacher appraisal. *Personal Relationships,* 141–158. http://dx.doi.org/10.1111/pere.12116 Retrieved March 18th, 2016.

Arbeit, M., Hershberg, R., Rubin, R., DeSouza, L., & Lerner, J. (2016). "I'm hoping that I can have better relationships": Exploring interpersonal connection for young men. *Qualitative Psychology, 3*(1), 79–97. http://dx.doi.org/10.1037/qup0000042 Retrieved March 18th, 2016.

Carbonneau, N., Vallerand, R., Lavigne, G., & Paquet, Y. (2016). "I'm not the same person since I met you": The role of romantic passion in how people change when they get involved in a romantic relationship. *Motivation and Emotion, 37,* 106–120. http://dx.doi.org/10.1007/s11031-015-9512-z Retrieved March 18th, 2016.

Carter, S. & Renshaw, K. (2016). Communication via different media during military deployment and post-deployment relationship satisfaction. *Military Behavioral Health,* 1–9. http://dx.doi.org/10.1080/21635781.2016.1153535 Retrieved March 18th, 2016.

Cavanaugh, A. & Buehler, C. (2016). Adolescent loneliness and social anxiety: The role of multiple sources of support. *Journal of Social and Personal Relationships,* 1–21. http://dx.doi.org/10.1177/0265407514567837 Retrieved March 18th, 2016.

Duncan, B., Miller, S., Wampold, B., & Hubble, M. (1999). *The heart & soul of change.* New York, NY: American Psychiatric Association.

Feeney, B. & Collins, N. (2014). A new look at social support: A theoretical perspective on thriving through relationships. *Personality and Social Psychology Review,* 1–35. http://dx.doi.org/10.1177/1088868314544222 Retrieved March 18th, 2016.

Fein, E. (2015). Making meaningful worlds: Role-playing subcultures and the autism spectrum. *Culture, Medicine and Psychiatry, 39*(2), 299–321. http://dx.doi.org/10.1007/s11013-015-9443-x Retrieved March 18th, 2016.

Firestone, L. (2009). Staying compatible by staying yourself. *Relationships: PsychAlive.* Retrieved March 1st, 2016 from http://www.psychalive.org/staying-compatible-by-staying-yourself/

Gottman, J. M. & Krokoff, L. J. (1989). Marital interaction and satisfaction: A longitudinal view. *Journal of Consulting in Clinical Psychology, 57*(1), 47–52. http://dx.doi.org/10.1037/0022-006X.57.1.47 Retrieved March 18th, 2016.

Gurman, A., Lebo, J., & Snyder, D. (2015). *Clinical handbook of couple therapy.* New York, NY: Guilford.

Kim, J., LaRose, R., & Peng, W. (2009). Loneliness as the cause and the effect of problematic Internet use: The relationship between Internet use and psychological well-being. *Cyberpsychology and Behavior, 12*(4), 451–455. http://dx.doi.org/10.1089/cpb.2008.0327 Retrieved March 18th, 2016.

Kojola, E. & Moen, P. (2016). No more lock-step retirement: Boomers' shifting meanings of work and retirement. *Journal of Aging Studies, 36,* 59–70. http://dx.doi.org/10.1016/j.jaging.2015.12.003 Retrieved March 18th, 2016.

Liao, J. & Brunner, E. (2016). Structural and functional measures of social relationships and quality of life among older adults. *Quality of Life Research, 25*(1), 153–164. http://dx.doi.org/10.1007/s11136-015-1052-1 Retrieved March 18th, 2016.

Madianou, M. (2016). Ambient co-presence: Transnational family practices in polymedia environments. *Global Networks, 16*(2), 183–201. http://dx.doi.org/10.1111/glob.12105 Retrieved March 18th, 2016.

Marraffa, M. & Paternoster, A. (2016). Disentangling the self: A naturalistic approach to narrative self-construction. *New Ideas in Psychology, 40,* 115–122. http://dx.doi.org/10.1016/j.newideapsych.2015.08.003 Retrieved March 18th, 2016.

Martoncik, M. & Loksa, J. (2016). Do world of warcraft (MMORPG) players experience less loneliness and social anxiety in online world (virtual environment) than in real world (offline)? *Computers in Human Behavior, 56,* 127–134. http://dx.doi.org/10.1016/j.chb.2015.11.035 Retrieved March 18th, 2016.

Miller, S. (2015). *The failure rate of psychotherapy: What it is and what we can do.* Retrieved March 1st, 2016 from http://www.scottdmiller.com/feedback-informed-treatment-fit/the-failure-rate-of-psychotherapy-what-it-is-and-what-we-can-do/

Pence, E. & Paymar, M. (1993). *Education groups for men who batter.* New York, NY: Springer.

Ryan, T. & Xenos, S. (2011). Who uses Facebook? An investigation into the relationship between the Big Five, shyness, narcissism, loneliness, and Facebook usage. *Computers in Human Behavior, 27,* 1658–1664. http://dx.doi.org/10.1016/j.chb.2011.02.004 Retrieved March 18th, 2016.

Siegel, D. (2010). *The mindful therapist.* New York, NY: Norton & Co.

Siegel, D. (2013). *Brainstorm.* New York, NY: Norton & Co.

Su, S., Pettit, G., & Erath, S. (2016). Peer relations, parental social coaching, and young adolescent social anxiety. *Journal of Applied Developmental Psychology, 42,* 89–97. http://dx.doi.org/10.1016/j.appdev.2015.11.007 Retrieved March 18th, 2016.

Velonis, A. (2016). "He never did anything you typically think of as abuse": Experiences with violence in controlling and non-controlling relationships in a non-agency sample of women. *Violence Against Women, Feb 2016,* 1–24. http://dx.doi.org/10.1177/1077801215618805 Retrieved March 18th, 2016.

6 Identity

▶ WHAT ARE *IDENTITY* CONCERNS?

Identity can be defined in a number of ways. The term is often used to explain the distinguishing characteristics of a person, including their values and life experiences, but may also describe how a particular person, or group of people, compare in relation to others. For the purposes of this text, identity is viewed as how one defines the self not only at the individual level, but also in reference to others and to the surrounding world. It follows that identity concerns are those for which the client is struggling with any aspect of their personal characteristics or sense of self; these concerns may be wide and varied.

The activities in this chapter focus on how identity is used to describe and define our self. It is important to note that clients may not present identity concerns explicitly, but rather they may bring other questions about motivation, belonging, or self-worth. Hearing some of the following—or similar—statements may be an indicator that the client could appreciate the interventions found in this chapter.

"Everybody else seems so put together."

When working through various life transitions, regardless of age, a client may experience difficulties in navigating *autonomy*, which speaks to one's ability to make choices independent of the influence of others. Comparison to others is common, and comparison to a peer group can serve to motivate and instigate change (Garcia, Tor, & Schiff, 2013). Comparison and reflection with peers also helps to clarify individual values and goals, which are foundations of identity (Poehnell & Amundson, 2011).

However, social comparisons may also minimize feelings of autonomy, in particular where the client does not feel confident or comfortable with their definition of self. In these cases, evaluating the self against others as a measure of success, intelligence, or attractiveness, while providing a framework for social norms, may be impractical. Further, the increased availability of online/social media and thus access to social comparisons may also present challenges to definitions of self (Vogel, Rose, Roberts, & Eckles, 2014). Thus, addressing the impact of social media and contextualizing perceptions versus realities can be important discussions to have with clients.

"It's so hard to think about not having (him/her/them) in my life."

When a client has experienced a personal loss, such as a relationship ending, a significant death, or loss of job, part of that experience may include questions about how the personal identity persists and who a person is without that significant relationship. A client may struggle to recognize persistent aspects of individual identity that still endure after the loss of the relational identity (Neimeyer, 2010). This struggle can allude to a lack of reflection on *core values*, or *core beliefs*. Exploring these essential characteristics, as well as individual experiences and hopes for the future, can offer a reconnection for the client to their individual and persistent identity.

"I've never really had the greatest confidence in myself. "

Three terms used to describe how a person perceives oneself include: *self-concept*, *self-esteem*, and *self-confidence*. Self-concept refers to descriptions and notions about oneself that, while personalized, tend to be factual or logical, such as "I play the drums" or "I am a student." Self-esteem attaches value and judgment to these descriptions, such as "I play the drums well" or "I am a bad student," while self-confidence denotes the likelihood of these descriptions being true, such as "I *can* play the drums well" or "I will *always* be a bad student." It is possible for both self-esteem and self-confidence notions to become part of a client's self-concept. When this happens, the client may experience doubts about their sense of self or future successes.

"I just don't know why I need to do this."

This statement, and similar difficulties connecting actions with attitudes, may be considered to be *existential* issues, which represent a challenge with *meaning-making* (Vos, Craig, & Cooper, 2015). Often heard regarding career, study, or relationship pursuits, issues of meaning-making could indicate a need to explore core values or beliefs. Clients who are looking at existential identity concerns also tend to benefit from having space within a session to explore these questions in a more conversational manner. In many of these cases, supporting clients by building context and additional perspectives around their choices can lead to the successful negotiation of meaning and a fuller appreciation of existential issues.

"I feel like I don't fit in."

Identity, while comprised of autonomy and individual meaning-making, is paradoxical in that it also includes a *sense of belonging.* Social experiences offer scenarios within which a person can situate oneself in a reflecting community, receiving feedback on identity and individual self-hood in the process. These reflections offer opportunities to think critically, attempt flexibility with core values and beliefs, and influence the attitudes of others. When effective, these experiences result in a sense of community. However, a client may struggle with this process and be supported with exploring the integration of personal beliefs into group or social beliefs. Note that additional discussion of identity as it relates to relationships can be found in Chapter Five: Relationships and Communication (page 127).

While not specifically discussed in the following interventions, *cultural identity* deserves a critical mention. Cultural identity refers to self-identification related to membership in an ethnic, racial, gender, or religious group that influences attitudes, beliefs, and self-concept, all of which can impact personal identity. Clarity in cultural identity has been positively associated with self-esteem and self-concept, with participation in culture-specific activities improving the sense of identity and belonging (Usborne & Taylor, 2010). The resource list at the end of this chapter includes titles that focus more specifically on cultural identity.

▶ RELEVANCE

Identity, and by extension how we see ourselves, can often be at the core of why a client is seeking support. Identity is important because it frames how we make meaning from our experiences and life situations. Connecting meaning, daily activities, and a sense of why we do what we do influences drive, purpose, and the ability to set goals and achieve them (Noble-Carr, Barker, & McArthur, 2013). A strong sense of self, in particular regarding autonomy, can lead to a feeling of agency within situations. By recognizing and taking ownership over certain aspects of their lives, clients build feelings of hope and confidence. In addition, defining and solidifying an understanding of self can contribute to a sense of belonging within a larger whole, which has been shown to lead to fuller and more enriching lives (Reich, Zautra, & Stuart Hall, 2010).

▶ WHAT WORKS WELL

The founding work on identity formation is often attributed to Erik Erikson, who, within a broader theory on psychosocial development, described a number of stages, each reached through the resolution of specific crises, such as trust versus mistrust, and intimacy versus isolation. Focusing on the conflicts and conditions inherent in these specific life tasks, Erikson believed that helping professionals' work includes supporting the client's resolution of these concerns by encouraging client strengths such as hope, purpose, and fidelity (Erikson, 1956).

James Marcia has looked specifically at adolescence, thought to be a key period of identity development. Marcia contends that, rather than stages, identity formation is better characterized by distinct statuses (Marcia, 1989). According to this theory, exploring commitment to a particular status, which may include religion or political values, can support the improvement of a client's identity concerns. Dan Siegel has also focused on adolescent development as a key period of identity exploration. Siegel suggests that behavioral characteristics interact closely with identity outcomes during adolescence. Creativity during adolescence, for instance, may result in identity characteristics persisting into adulthood, including flexibility and abstractions (Siegel, 2013).

Though not solely focused on identity, Self-Determination Theory (Deci & Ryan, 2011) emphasizes the roles that intrinsic and extrinsic motivation play in how we interact with our environment, with significant attention given to ideas of autonomy and awareness of personal choices. Self-Determination Theory places significance on the development of client goals within counseling contexts and has influenced a number of modern-day counseling techniques, such as those found in Motivational Interviewing (Miller & Rollnick, 2013).

Some of the interventions contained in this chapter use reframing or reauthoring scenarios as a foundation for exploring identity and beliefs about the self. These concepts are adapted from Narrative Therapy. Narrative Therapy invites the client to reconstruct self-concept through evaluating and reauthoring portions of their life narrative, highlighting strength- and hope-based personality characteristics and considering how those characteristics might be used in future scenarios toward a values-based life (White, 2007).

▶ FUTURE RESEARCH

Despite identity and its development being integral to many client concerns, the literature and research looking at practical interventions which focus on identity is surprisingly sparse (Syed & McLean, 2015). Much of the research that is available focuses on adolescence and early adulthood, which many agree is the period of life during which primary identities are formed. However, older adults still present with identity concerns; more research on identity and sense of self during adulthood is certainly needed.

How a person's identity has formed may also impact how effective different counseling strategies and frameworks may be, though this is currently unknown. For example, if external factors (such as family relationships or natural disasters in childhood) have had an influence on early stages of identity formation, does this change the effectiveness of counseling compared to identity formation that has been more internally driven? Related to this, while there are definite links between identity and the concept of resilience, what are the contributing factors to building individual resilience as it relates to shifting identities through the lifetime? Additionally, while some research has looked at the psychological factors of identity development, the role of the physical body has not yet been connected to identity; this relationship could benefit from exploration.

Finally, there needs to be a call toward more concrete and evidence-driven data on the effectiveness of different counseling frameworks when working with identity concerns. The effectiveness of Narrative Therapy bears particular consideration, as the idea of reframing at its heart seems to connect well with defining oneself, but this notion has yet to be thoroughly tested.

▶ INTERVENTIONS IN THIS CHAPTER

Psychoeducational

Multiple Identities (page 162): This short activity gets clients thinking about expanding their own identity-based belief system.

Talk-Based/Motivational

Be You for a Day (page 165): This intervention invites the client to focus on the best traits represented in their self-concept.

Art-Based

Downs and Ups (page 168): This intervention invites the client to identify five personal or historic events that have influenced the client's sense of self.

Hands-On

Letter to Future Self (page 171): This intervention invites the client to consider the continuity of personal characteristics and imagined future-self.

Relational

Five Favorites (page 174): This intervention invites the client to identify the client's personal likes, positive aspects of the self, and what memories and experiences one owns.

Group

Hot Potato (page 177): In this high-energy game, group members get to know each other by answering identity questions.

Homework

Life as a Story (page 180): This narrative-based homework is designed to reframe the way in which a client currently thinks about their life.

▶ MULTIPLE IDENTITIES

AMOUNT OF TIME

15–20 minutes

MATERIALS NEEDED

- Paper (optional)
- Pen or markers (optional)

Type of Activity

Psychoeducational

Intent/Used for . . .

This activity educates the client on the notion of multiple identities, and in turn can help the client recognize their own multiple identities. This recognition can be very useful for clients who are feeling stuck or trapped in a particular aspect of their lives, and also may be used to identify strengths in one identity that may not typically be considered in other identities.

Step-by-Step Instructions

1. Begin the discussion by focusing in on one identity of the client—ideally, it is one that they have previously mentioned or are bringing up often in-session. For example, the client may talk about being a romantic partner a number of times when discussing relationships.
2. Ask the client to think about their identity (in this case, as a 'romantic partner'), and to list, either out loud or on paper, all of the qualities and characteristics that are associated with that identity. It is useful to have them complete the sentence "[Identity] is . . ." (for example, "A romantic partner is . . .").
3. Explain to the client that there is a concept around people having 'multiple identities.' This does not mean the same thing as multiple personalities! Rather, individuals can identify as belonging to more than one label and/or group. So, for example, the client who is currently

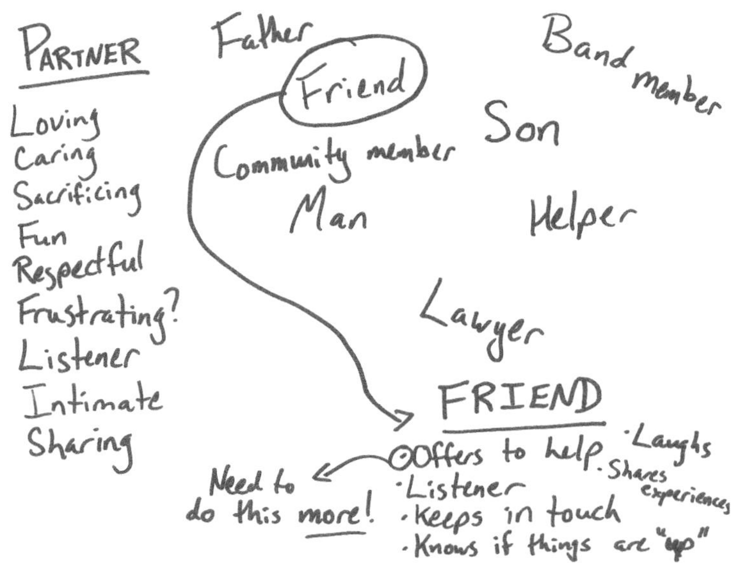

Figure 6.1 Once a client gets started on recognizing different identities, it can be difficult to stop.

looking at their identity as a 'romantic partner,' and all that entails, may also identify as a 'friend'—not necessarily at the same time, but most individuals, in this sense, have the capacity to have more than one identity.

4. Have the client list as many different identities as they can with which they feel they can associate (an 'identity list').
5. Reflect that we don't often take the time to appreciate the multiple and varied identities that we have within ourselves—occasionally, we may get caught up in trying to be/exist in only one of the identities.
6. Have the client select one of their listed identities that they feel they haven't been connecting with recently, or one that doesn't often get much attention. Ask the client to make a different list of qualities and characteristics, this time using the new/neglected identity.
7. Take some time to reflect on any similarities or differences between the two lists.
8. If appropriate/applicable, ask the client to identify one major strength that is associated with each identity on their identity list. Discuss with the client how some of these strengths, typically associated with one identity, may be useful in addressing issues that are arising in another identity.

Guiding Questions

- How do you think your (family/friends/partner) would answer some of these questions about your identity?
- I wonder if there are ways in which this quality, which you are seeing in a negative light, can actually be positive or useful. What do you think is the benefit of having this quality?
- Are there times when one identity blends with another identity? What does that look like? Are there advantages to this?
- What would be the advantage to having different identities?
- How will you remind yourself of some of these strengths over the next few days?

Tips/Ways to Change

- This can be adapted to younger ages—it is often useful when doing so to look at the different environments (ex. school, home, with friends, etc.), rather than talking about the more internally based identity concepts. Most children are able to identify how they sometimes change behaviors when interacting with different people or in different places.
- Using sticky notes for listing both the different identities and the qualities/characteristics can allow for some fun ways to make the activity a bit more hands-on—the client can actually move around different characteristics to create a 'merged' identity, or can physically move some of the strengths/desired characteristics from one identity to another, which can be very empowering.
- Depending on the nature of the client's intent in coming to therapy, it may be useful to have a discussion around how some of the qualities/characteristics have changed for specific identities throughout the years.
- Similarly, it is possible to have a discussion around a client's ideal/desired identity, versus the real/experienced identity.
- This activity flows quite nicely into the 'Be You for a Day' intervention, found on page 165.

NOTES

▶ BE YOU FOR A DAY

Type of Activity

Talk-based/Motivational

AMOUNT OF TIME

10–15 minutes

MATERIALS NEEDED

- Paper (optional)
- Pen or markers (optional)

Intent/Used for . . .

This activity takes advantage of the psychoeducation from Multiple Identities (page 162), though it is possible to complete this activity without the client having the Multiple Identities background. Be You for a Day allows the client to focus in on selected, positive aspects of themselves, which in turn can guide future identity-related decisions and lessen the sometimes overwhelming feelings that come in times of transition and change.

Step-by-Step Instructions

1. Ask the client about their familiarity with 'Be _____ for a Day' contests, such as 'Be the president for a day' or 'Be principal for a day.'
2. If the client is unfamiliar with the concept, explain in brief:
   - People pay money or have tickets for a chance to win 24 hours in another person's role—typically, the winner will not be able to enact lasting change in the role, but will be given most of the bonuses and perks associated with it.
3. Have the client describe their ideal 'Be ______ for a Day' contest—who/what would they want to be for 24 hours? What would they do during those 24 hours?
4. (This step is optional and is best included when clients have prior knowledge of Multiple Identities.) Have the client list a few of the different roles that they enact from day to day, in particular emphasizing/thinking about the ones which other people may be interested in 'being' for a day. (This is the reverse of step 3.)
5. Ask the client to pick one, and only one, role or aspect of themselves that, if they had the chance, they would want to focus on/be for 24 hours.
   - This focus would *not* come at the cost of losing other aspects/identities, and there would be no lasting negative consequences.
   - This can be a difficult step for clients, and therefore it may be useful for the helping professional to suggest possibilities.
6. Have the client list the things that they would do in the 24-hour period of focusing solely on that identity/role—as exhaustive as possible!
7. Briefly address the reality that other identity roles or aspects may still be present, but ask the client to select three of the things that they listed that they think may be possible to do over the following week (or 24 hours, if that is more applicable).
8. Invite the client to develop action items around the three possibilities selected.

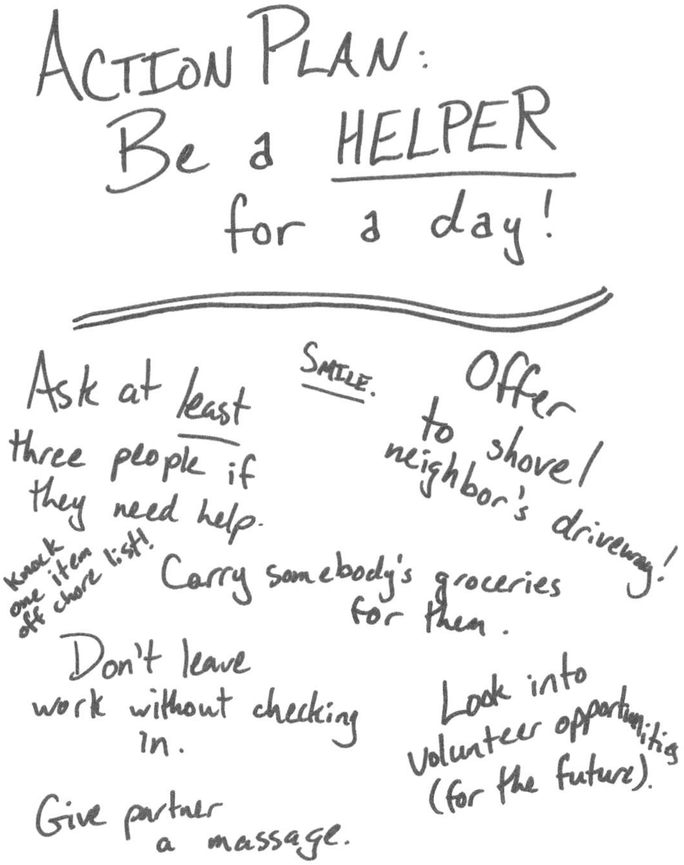

Figure 6.2 We do not often consider ourselves as somebody others look up to—imagine a world where we all saw ourselves as having desirable traits.

Guiding Questions

- Why are 'Be ______ for a Day' contests so popular?
- What is the draw in being somebody else, or taking somebody else's role?
- Why are these contests for only 24 hours? Are there disadvantages to a longer timeframe?
- Sometimes it's difficult to focus on just this one aspect/'hat'—what types of things might help in those difficult times?
- How does this activity fit with some of the questions or concerns you have been sharing in-session?

Tips/Ways to Change

- When the helping professional is working with younger children, simplifying choices by talking about three or four scenarios where they may act or 'be' different (for example, at school, with family relations, with friends, in a store, etc.) may help with understanding the concepts. Young people may need additional guidance in thinking about step 7.

- It is possible to present this activity as a lead into homework: invite the client to choose or be one of the aspects or roles for the next day.
- Invite the client to create a poster advertising the 'Be (the client) for a Day' contest.
- Set a regular date (e.g. the 15th of every month) for which the client will choose one aspect to emphasize for the duration of that day, each time choosing something different.

NOTES

DOWNS AND UPS

AMOUNT OF TIME

20–25 minutes

MATERIALS NEEDED

- Paper
- Crayons or colored pencils
- Whiteboard and markers (optional)

Type of Activity

Art-based

Intent/Used for . . .

This activity invites the client to identify five personal or historical events that have influenced the client's sense of self. Through this, Downs and Ups explores how external events influence characteristics of identity. This activity proves helpful for individuals who are having difficulties connecting life events to personal characteristics, or making meaning out of present-day choices based on historical experiences and outcomes.

Step-by-Step Instructions

1. Invite the client to consider three 'ups' and two 'downs' that they have experienced over their lifetime. If the client is having difficulty coming up with ideas, the helping professional can offer examples or possibilities.
   - 'Ups' are pleasant or positive experiences, such as meeting a new friend, a meaningful achievement, or an exciting trip or relocation.
   - 'Downs' are when things seemed particularly challenging or low, and the client used personality strengths and skills to move through these events.
2. Discuss how these events, both downs and ups, represent moments in time when we might consider how our lives would be different if they had not happened. These were also moments that required us to access our skills to manage the moment or episode.

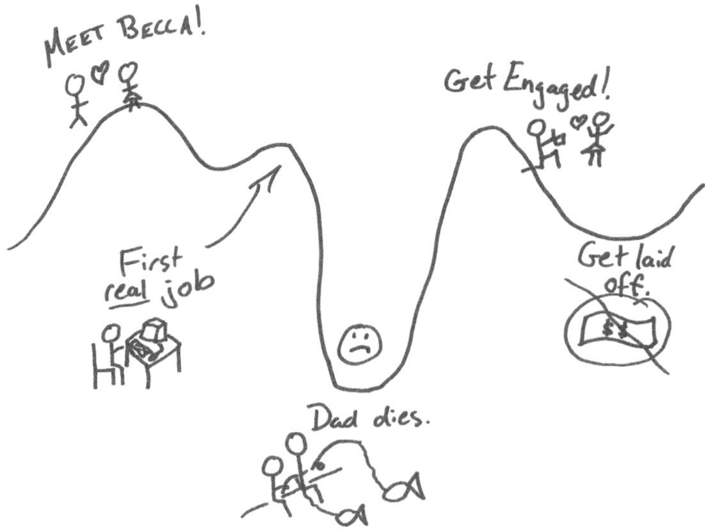

Figure 6.3 An invitation to explore events that have been critical to the client's sense of self—what themes arise in the timeline?

3. Offer encouragement during this discussion; this is quite a thoughtful and challenging activity, with some clients having difficulty considering three ups and two downs, and others possibly having difficulty choosing *only* this number.
4. Invite the client to draw a wavy line with three peaks and two valleys, and to represent the identified three ups and two downs on paper, however it feels suitable. This could include words or images. I typically allow clients between five to 15 minutes for art creation in order to reduce over-thinking and allow the appropriate amount of time for discussion.
5. Allow the client to reflect on the experience. If time is limited, simply ask the client what stood out from the activity.
6. Explore how and if these incidents influenced the client's sense of self, and reflect on different internal and external experiences that influence changes in the sense of self. If appropriate for client concerns or needs, invite the client to imagine future internal/external events that may influence the sense of self, such as graduation or retirement.
7. Invite the client to identify one aspect of this activity that the counselor should remember *first*, given that these are important aspects of the client's personal history and identity development.

Guiding Questions

- What can you tell me about what you've created?
- Did you know any of the responses right away?
- How did this/these incident(s) shape you in a meaningful way? Did any of these events influence a decision you made today? This week? This month?
- What would someone know about you, your characteristics, and your identity by looking at this?
- What is one thing you would hope that I remember or know about your identity by seeing this creation?

Tips/Ways to Change

- More or fewer Ups or Downs can be used as time permits.
- Care should be taken when exploring critical life incidents with someone who has experienced trauma(s), with appropriate safety measures, grounding strategies, and consultation available.
- *Insignificants*: An alternate activity is to invite the client to identify Downs and Ups that were seemingly insignificant at the time but that, upon reflection, were turning points for the client. This activity is particularly useful when working in trauma healing, as there is an opportunity to invite the client to explore other life events that played a role in current strengths and resiliencies, and to further reconnect the client to the present and their whole life.
- *See the Future:* A response or follow-up activity could include an invitation to see two Ups and one Down in the future, integrating the discussion of internal and external changes that influence the client's life experience and identity and flexibility toward adapting to events or the never-ending process of change that happens with ourselves and the world.

NOTES

▶ LETTER TO FUTURE SELF

Type of Activity

Hands-on

AMOUNT OF TIME

5–15 minutes

MATERIALS NEEDED

- Paper
- Pen
- Computer (optional)
- Stationary (optional)

Intent/Used for . . .

This activity encourages connecting the client with the future self and aspects of the identity that may continue. It also encourages the client to consider the ongoing process of change.

Step-by-Step Instructions

1. Invite the client to consider the changing self. Reflect on who the client was five to 10 years ago, or even one year ago. Explore, if appropriate, the concept of a growing and changing self, while including reflection on persistent characteristics that allow us to continue into the future and reflect backward on our lives.
2. Invite the client to consider the future self, keeping in mind how things may be different or the same now as they were 10 years, five years, or one year ago.
3. Invite the client to write a letter to their imagined future self, keeping persistent parts of the self in mind while also acknowledging how we change.
4. If the client is struggling, consider offering a structure of a greeting, one or two sentences about what is happening at this point in the client's life, one or two sentences acknowledging the person's strengths, and one sentence to imagine what they might want to hear or be reminded of in the future. I also encourage clients to close the letter with a respectful endearment, such as "Warm regards."
5. Discussion after this activity is not always necessary, but if relevant, the therapist might invite the client to consider where they think they might be in the future, what they will have overcome, and how it will feel to read their own letter of encouragement.

Guiding Questions

- There is a level of sacredness to writing a note to the self, and often this activity is profoundly personal. I do not generally question clients after this activity unless they would like to speak about the note, except to thank them for participating and encouraging their future self.

Tips/Ways to Change

- Stationary or notecards are a nice gesture for this activity.
- There are a number of online resources (such as www.futureme.org) where an e-mail can be typed.
- Alternates could include letters to others, letters to those who are absent, letters to one's higher power, or gratitude notes to the self.

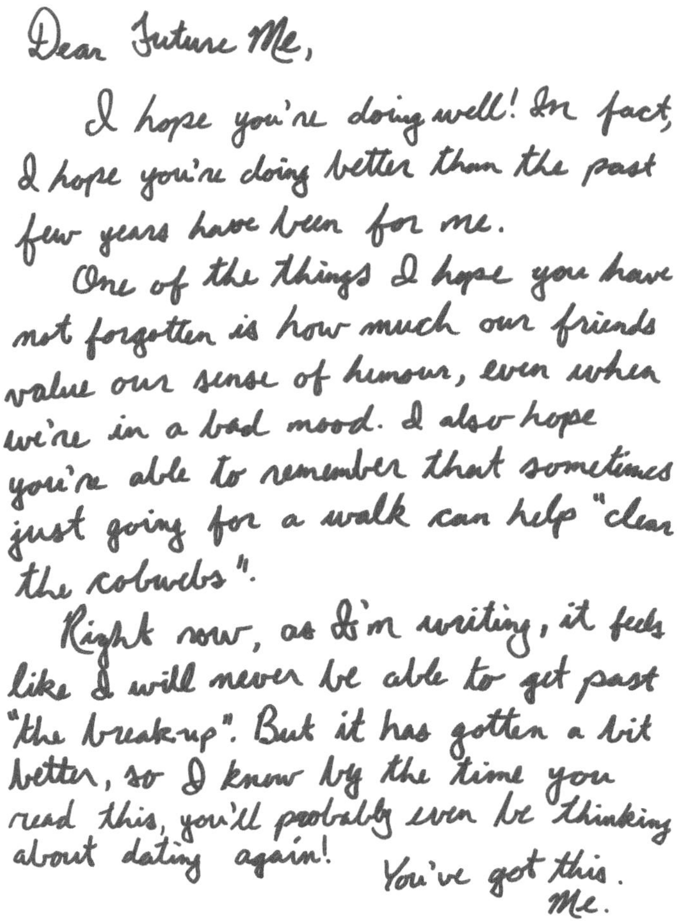

Dear Future Me,

I hope you're doing well! In fact, I hope you're doing better than the past few years have been for me.

One of the things I hope you have not forgotten is how much our friends value our sense of humour, even when we're in a bad mood. I also hope you're able to remember that sometimes just going for a walk can help "clear the cobwebs".

Right now, as I'm writing, it feels like I will never be able to get past "the break-up". But it has gotten a bit better, so I know by the time you read this, you'll probably even be thinking about dating again!

You've got this.

Me.

Figure 6.4 A letter to the self offers a future orientation and encourages acknowledgment and positive self-talk.

- One of my favorite therapy closing activities is a letter to the self, a thank-you note, which the client takes with them and opens in case of emergency, when they might need to remember all of the hard work that they did and access their own resilience and strength to move forward or to seek help if necessary.

NOTES

FIVE FAVORITES

AMOUNT OF TIME

10–15 minutes

MATERIALS NEEDED

- Paper (optional)
- Pen or markers (optional)

Type of Activity

Relational

Intent/Used for . . .

This activity works well for early in the counseling relationship as a way to get to know the client. It also provides space for the client to name specific pleasant ideas that are 'owned' by the client, while engaging the client in encouraging positive memories. This activity can also support self-soothing and emotion regulation, as described below in Tips/Ways to Change.

Step-by-Step Instructions

1. Use paper and pen (or crayon) to document the client's responses. Ensure the client can see what you are writing and list the five senses down the page, leaving a space beside each so the client can anticipate their participation. The five senses are: scent, sound, taste, touch, sight.
2. Explain that this activity works toward getting a balanced knowledge of the client (for both the client and the helping professional), and also offers the client a list of positive sensory events that they can keep with them.
3. Invite the client to reflect on sensory memory. Acknowledge the power of fearful, anxious, or angry experiences which may have resulted in their seeking counseling. Validate that the client has also experienced a number of positive events that have influenced memories.
4. Begin with an invitation to consider the sense of smell. Invite the client to name one of their favorite smells. At first, a client might find this to be rather challenging. Encourage the client by describing some things that might be common, such as a smell from nature, the smell of cooking or baking, or a favorite soap. Care should be taken not to overwhelm the client with choices, with suggestions only being offered if the client is struggling. Use one or two words to label what the client has recalled. Acknowledge and validate the client's choice. Invite the client to further expand on that memory, if desired.
5. Continue with sound. Again, if necessary, encourage the client by offering suggestions, such as sounds from nature or a piece of music or particular instrument. Validate and encourage the client's options. Invite the client to further discuss and reflect on this sensory memory if the client is interested.
6. Continue with taste and touch, using one or two descriptive words to add to the list as the client shares.
7. I prefer to save a visual memory for the final memory, as this can sometimes paradoxically encompass all five senses. Invite the client to explore this memory deeply, describing the visual space, real or imagined, in detail. If it is appropriate at this time, invite the client to attempt to engage other senses while describing the visual memory.
8. Use immediacy. Invite the client to reflect on what is noticed in the body and mind after spending time with these sensory experiences. Reflect on the importance of these memories and the sense of a complete self, offering balance to unpleasant or negative experiences that might be interfering with the client's life at present.

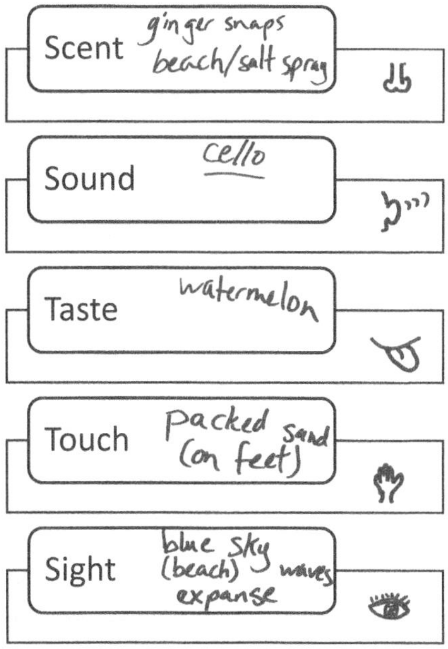

Figure 6.5 Sensory memories are generally attached to meaningful stories and events.

9. If the client shows interest in expanding this activity, invite them to expand the list to include two or three additional pleasant sensory experiences as a homework activity. Encourage memories that are simple, such as fresh air upon leaving the office, or the feel of warmth from putting on a sweatshirt.

Guiding Questions

- Do you consider these things often?
- How have these sensory preferences changed over time?
- Which sense was the hardest for you to think about? Which was the easiest?
- Did this activity get easier as we spent more time with it?
- Why do you think that these sensory memories are important to who you are as a person? Do you think these are the same or different from other people?
- What do you see as the connection between these pleasant sensory images and your identity/current concerns?

Tips/Ways to Change

- Stay mindful of different abilities to determine whether the client is able to engage all five senses. This activity is easily adaptable to two or three senses.
- This activity can be used to encourage the use of visual imagery for self-soothing and emotion regulation. Discuss the use of the client's list as an 'in case of emergency' list should they need reminding of their pleasant sensory memories, or to take a short break in a safe place that they carry in their memory.
- Invite the client to reflect on times they might have used daydreaming as a self-soothing strategy, and encourage the use of pleasant sensory memory as intentional daydreaming.

NOTES

▶ HOT POTATO

Type of Activity

Group

AMOUNT OF TIME

10–15 minutes

Intent/Used for . . .

A popular children's game has been adapted here for a quick, high-energy group intervention. The activity invites participants to answer questions about their individual identity characteristics, or shared characteristics, to group-mates, using prompts from the group facilitator. This activity is useful for generating thoughts about individual characteristics and also gaining insight through listening to the examples of others' individual characteristics.

MATERIALS NEEDED

- Ball
- Stereo/computer
- Speakers
- Sandbag (optional)

Step-by-Step Instructions

1. Invite group members to sit or stand in a circle. I prefer standing for this activity, but sitting in a circle would be just as easy.
2. Place index cards with questions in the center of the circle (suggestions for possible questions are included in the following section).
3. Instruct the participants that the group will be playing Hot Potato. Explain that Hot Potato is a very old game in which a ball is passed around, and when the music stops, the person holding the ball is responsible for answering a question written on an index card.
4. Begin the game by starting the music and passing around a ball, small sandbag, or any other handheld object. Invite the participants to either pass the ball to the person next to them, or to toss the ball back and forth across the circle while the music plays.

Figure 6.6 Keep the ball moving through the group, answering questions about identity.

- If the facilitator is using the Hot Potato toy, the music will stop randomly as programmed into the toy. If the facilitator is using their own music, the facilitator will be responsible for stopping the music at random intervals or deciding otherwise how to time the music for game play.

5. When the music stops, the participant holding the ball (the 'Hot Potato') is responsible for answering a question from an index card chosen from the center of the circle. All of the questions focus on identity. When the music stops, the person holding the Hot Potato is invited to choose a card from the pile in the center of the circle, read the question aloud, and answer the question.
6. Take a moment to validate what the person has said and acknowledge that they shared. Perhaps connect the question by asking if anyone else in the group shares that same quality or wishes that they had that same quality. The participant who answered the question may then start the next Hot Potato round.
7. Continue the game until everyone has had a chance to answer a question. For a group with 10 participants, this typically takes about 10 minutes.

Guiding Questions

(Note: These are questions to print on the Hot Potato cards.)

- Name a place you feel relaxed.
- What is one place that you have always wanted to travel to?
- If your last name (family name) was a word that described you, what would it be?
- How old do you feel?
- What is one topic you always wanted to learn about?
- Describe one thing you like about yourself.
- How would your favorite friend or family member describe you?
- Finish this sentence: "Saying goodbye is . . ."
- Finish this sentence: "Saying hello is . . ."
- Use three words to describe yourself.
- What is your favorite season of the year?
- What animal would make your best companion?
- What is one thing you would like to build?
- What living famous person do you think would be cool to hang out with?
- What song do you listen to when you want to feel happy?
- Who inspires you?
- What are you excited about?
- When you were a little kid, what did you want to be when you were grown up?
- What is the first thing you do when you wake up?
- What do you want to be when you are grown up?
- Who do you look up to?
- What is one thing in your life that you are most grateful for?
- What are three things that you appear to have in common with other group member(s)?

Tips/Ways to Change

- I like to do this at the start of the group, and then at the end of the group. While suggestions for questions are offered, it is not difficult to adapt the questions based on the specific needs of your group.
- I like to revisit this game at the end of the group, and this time invite the participants to ask identity questions of their own, or name something that stands out about the group. This requires additional facilitation and holding the space by the group facilitator; however, it is a really interesting way for participants to share and receive feedback about how they participated in the group.
- You may also separate the questions to be placed in front of each group member, one question each; or as the facilitator, you might simply ask the question rather than have the participants read the question from a question card.
- In her book *Creative Interventions for Children and Youth*, Liana Lowenstein (1999) offers an alternate to this Hot Potato activity by encouraging awareness and expression of feelings.
- Many toy stores sell a Hot Potato game, a device that comes with its own randomized timer, which can be substituted for the ball or sandbag.
- There are many ways to modify this activity, either by changing the questions, or by using an icebreaker/conversation starter ball (such as those available at www.thumball.com).

NOTES

LIFE AS A STORY

AMOUNT OF TIME

Explanation: 10 minutes

Debrief: 30 minutes

MATERIALS NEEDED

- Paper (optional)
- Pen or markers (optional)

Type of Activity

Homework

Intent/Used for . . .

This homework allows the client to explore their life as a metaphor and can be useful for identifying various aspects of his/her self-concept. In particular, the 'Life Story' can be used to explore relationships in the client's life and how the client perceives their own sense of belonging. Depending on the follow-up debrief/discussion, clients may also gain greater awareness and clarity of counseling goals. I especially like to use this homework for clients who are having difficulty articulating specific aspects of their goals/issues.

Step-by-Step Instructions

1. Determine what story metaphor framework would work best for the client—a book/novel, a movie, or possibly even a video game or piece of music. This can be done in the initial stages of the session, while developing rapport (Is the client a reader? Do they prefer movies more?)
2. For the homework, ask the client to think about their life 'as if it were a [book/movie/etc.].'
3. Provide prompting questions, such as:
   - What genre would it be (mystery/adventure/comedy/tragedy/etc.)?
   - Who are the characters in the story? The main character(s)? The background and supporting characters?
   - What roles do the characters play (including the client)?
   - Where is the story headed—a struggle leading to a happy ending, a continuous journey, the next 'level,' etc.?
   - Where is the story currently at—the beginning or end of a chapter, close to the climax, etc.?
4. It is optional for the client to write down their thoughts; however, tell them that you will be following up with this story in the next session.

Debrief

1. Ask the client to describe their life story, as per the homework (do not give too much direction here). Even if they have not completed it, encourage this as a safe space/time to think about it.
2. With older clients in particular, ask how the process of developing their story was for them, and if there are any insights that they would be willing to share.
3. Take some time to explore the characters and the roles they play—keep an eye out for talking points, specifically around the client as the main character, 'missing' elements or characters yet to come, and any 'villains' and how they are being dealt with.

Figure 6.7 Appeal to the client's sense of creativity and watch the story grow.

Guiding Questions

- When you think about stories, what types of stories appeal to you—mysteries, fantasy, etc.?
- Sometimes people think about their own lives as a type of story that is still unfolding—what do you think of that?

Debrief

- Are there other stories that you would *like* your life story to be like?
- Are there any missing characters, or characters who have yet to make an appearance?
- What role(s) do these characters provide in the story? Are there any roles that multiple characters serve?
- What is exciting/daunting about the upcoming chapter?

Tips/Ways to Change

- As mentioned, it is integral to tailor the framework to the client—if a client talks about video games quite a bit, use that!
- Pay attention to the genre chosen by the client—sometimes this can be useful in recognizing 'missing' elements in the story. For example, if a client says their life is a 'journey/adventure' type story, these typically have map-related elements—who provides the map for the client?
- The debrief part of this activity tends to be the more powerful component—with this in mind, try to emphasize the fun of the homework part.
- Continue to check in with the client in future sessions regarding their life as a story, if this is something that seems appealing to them.
- Having paper and markers/crayons in front of the client during the debrief can be very useful if they find a visual explanation more appropriate.

NOTES

▶ OTHER RESOURCES

Brown, B. (2007). *I thought it was just me (but it isn't).* New York, NY: Gotham.

Duran, E. & Duran, B. (1995). *Postcolonial psychology.* New York, NY: SUNY.

Eleftheriadou, Z. (2010). *Psychotherapy and culture: Weaving inner and outer worlds.* London: Karnac Books Ltd.

Elliott, A. (2011). *Routledge handbook of identity studies.* New York, NY: Routledge.

Killerman, S. (2013). *The social justice advocate's handbook: A guide to gender.* Austin, TX: Impetus.

Lawler, S. (2007). *Identity: Sociological perspectives.* Cambridge: Polity.

Lindholm, C. (2007). *Culture and identity: The history, theory, and practice of psychological anthropology.* Oxford, England: Oxford.

Lowenstein, L. (1999). *Creative interventions for troubled children and youth.* Toronto, ON: Champion Press.

McLean, K. C. & Syed, M. (Eds.). (2015). *The Oxford handbook of identity development.* New York, NY: Oxford.

Poehnell, G. & Amundson, N. E. (2011). *Hope-filled engagement.* Richmond, BC: Ergon.

Siegel, D. (2013). *Brainstorm.* New York, NY: Penguin.

▶ REFERENCES

Deci, E. L. & Ryan, R. M. (2011). Self-determination theory. In P. A. M. Van Lange, A. W. Kruglanski, & E. T. Higgins (Eds.), *The handbook of theories of social psychology*, Vol. 1. (416–437). London: Sage.

Erikson, E. H. (1956). The problem of ego identity. *Journal of the American Psychoanalytic Association, 4*, 56–121. http://dx.doi.org/10.1177/000306515600400104 Retrieved January 16th, 2016.

Garcia, S. M., Tor, A., & Schiff, T. M. (2013). The psychology of competition: A social comparison perspective. *Perspectives on Psychological Science, 8*(6), 634–650. http://dx.doi.org/10.1177/1745691613504114 Retrieved January 16th, 2016.

Marcia, J. E. (1989). Identity and intervention. *Journal of Adolescence, 12*(4), 401–410. http://dx.doi.org/10.1016/0140-1971(89)90063-8 Retrieved January 16th, 2016.

Miller, W. R. & Rollnick, S. (2013). *Motivational interviewing: Helping people change* (3rd ed.). New York, NY: Guilford Press.

Neimeyer, R. A. (2010). Searching for the meaning of meaning: Grief therapy and the process of reconstruction. *Death Studies, 24*(6), 541–548. http://dx.doi.org/10.1080/07481180050121480 Retrieved January 16th, 2016.

Noble-Carr, D., Barker, J., & McArthur, M. (2013). *Me, myself, and I: Identity and meaning in the lives of vulnerable young people.* Canberra: Institute of Child Protection Studies.

Poehnell, G. & Amundson, N. E. (2011). *Hope-filled engagement.* Richmond, BC: Ergon.

Reich, J. W., Zautra, A. J., & Stuart Hall, J. (Eds.). (2010). *Handbook of adult resilience.* New York, NY: Guilford.

Siegel, D. (2013). *Brainstorm.* New York, NY: Penguin.

Syed, M. & McLean, K. C. (2015). The future of identity development research: Reflections, tensions, and challenges. In K. C. McLean & M. Syed (Eds.), *The Oxford handbook of identity development* (562–574). New York, NY: Oxford.

Usborne, E. & Taylor, D. (2010). The role of cultural identity clarity for self-concept clarity, self-esteem, and subjective well-being. *Personality and Social Psychology Bulletin, 36*(7), 883–897. http://dx.doi.org/10.1177/0146167210372215 Retrieved February 7th, 2016.

Vogel, E. A., Rose, J. P., Roberts, L. R., & Eckles, K. (2014). Social comparison, social media, and self-esteem. *Psychology of Popular Media Culture, 3*(4), 206–222. http://dx.doi.org/10.1037/ppm0000047 Retrieved February 6th, 2016.

Vos, J., Craig, M., & Cooper, M. (2015). Existential therapies: A meta-analysis of their effects on psychological outcomes. *Journal of Consulting and Clinical Psychology, 83*(1), 115–128. http://dx.doi.org/10.1037/a0037167 Retrieved January 16th, 2016.

White, M. (2007). *Maps of narrative practices.* New York, NY: W. W. Norton & Company.

7 Endings

▶ WHAT ARE *ENDINGS*?

Endings are integral threads woven throughout the counseling process. Session-by-session, helping professionals are tasked with timekeeping, finding a natural or useful stopping point, and somehow summarizing how time was spent in a meaningful way. Clients *or* counselors may transfer, relocate, or graduate from services at any given time. Initial intake sessions may even include a discussion of limits to the number of sessions, introducing an ending before counseling has truly begun.

While grief may be associated with endings, this chapter is not meant to address the deep sorrow and anguish that may be associated with an unexpected or despairing loss. Rather, this chapter aims to explore the endings inherent in counseling transitions: movement between one state into another, shifting from one activity to another, or recognizing a final point and stopping. The activities in the following pages are not strictly considered interventions, as they are not designed to elicit any particular behavioral changes, unlike the interventions found in the previous chapters. Rather, these activities are intended to invite an openness to the experience of change, transition, or closing associated with endings in helping services. The focus within these pages is toward guiding a conversation around change and collaboratively identifying a natural ending point. Change can be difficult, and you may hear this or other phrases explored in this chapter when introducing these conversations to clients:

"What if I still need help after six sessions?"

Limits to client sessions are often a necessity, whether because of organizational policy, managed care, or caseload and wait-listing concerns. When the helping professional is beginning the helping process, it is important to fully inform the client, from the outset, of what can be expected. This may be through information found in a brochure, or as part of a separate intake session. However, it is important for clients to know at the *beginning* of counseling when the end can be anticipated; client expectations of how the counseling process will unfold influence client engagement and relationship development with the counselor (Owen, Smith, & Rodolfa, 2009). Further, this discussion invites collaboration with the client as to how they might best use those sessions. This may include practical facets, such as planning how often the client would like to attend.

A discussion on limits to sessions also invites the client to discuss counseling in terms of *pieces of work*. An honest discussion with a client about specific, identifiable, and experienced concerns helps to focus the session and provide an agenda for each following session. While these limits may not seem appropriate for someone healing from long-term or ongoing concerns, or a person with a persistent mental health concern, the helping professional is typically responsible for supporting a specific identified change or insight. This is particularly true where session limits are organizational policy, but also invites the client to consider what concerns are priority, as well as what currently presents the most urgency.

While it may feel challenging to discuss limits to sessions at the start of the counseling process, preparing to end is a relevant and reinforcing message. This may be a client's first experience considering themselves without the problem. A discussion about endings and limits invites conversations about therapeutic change, and how small shifts will influence the client's life. Further, it opens a dialogue on what happens when counseling is completed. Connections to natural or community resources may be discussed as options for where support and helpful relationships may be generated after the current sessions have finished.

"It is so hard to imagine what happens next."

Ending the therapeutic relationship may be attached to *other changes* that the client is experiencing, such as graduation, relocation, or perhaps a transfer of support services. This transition may prove difficult to navigate, as the client may experience anxiety and fear along with the anticipation of the change.

It is important to validate these changes and the experience of the unknown. In ending the helping process, a discussion of client strengths or skills that have been evidenced throughout the sessions will help to soothe some of these fears. Further, naming and processing the experience affirms the emotional experience of this ending and allows the client to determine their plans for managing their feelings. Small, manageable next steps offer an acknowledgment of the challenge and reinforce the notion that the client has the ability to move forward with change.

"Nothing has changed—if anything, it is worse."

Ending with a client is a challenge, both for the client and the helping professional. While it may be difficult to hear that a client is *frustrated or angry* about received services, it is important to acknowledge the intention under these types of statements and confirm those intentions with the client. Whether the ending is natural and planned, or abrupt and unexpected, the client may express their dissatisfaction with the termination, or the services in general.

Professional self-location and grounding skills should be engaged when listening to the client in this way. While we, the helping professionals, may feel compelled to defend the practice or our relationship skills and blame lack of movement, change, or insight on the client, in these moments of client discussion, we must return to our original reflective practice by acknowledging and affirming the client's ability and right to gain the services that are desired. Perhaps the client's frustration stems from closing and their sense of loss, resulting in a pulling back from the relationship. On the other hand, it is important to recognize that the client may be truly feeling as though they have somehow lost skills while attending counseling.

Inviting the client to explore their experience, expectations, and desires for the helping process—even if unfulfilled—provides an avenue for future work. This might include documenting with the client what they would want from their next helper, or from natural or community resources. If a client is closing due to monetary or managed care concerns, it might be appropriate to connect the client with local community supports, an ombudsperson, or another advocate in the area.

▶ RELEVANCE

A counseling relationship is unique in that it begins so that it may end. Attending counseling is an attempt for a client to identify and resolve issues that proved a challenge and required additional supports. Connecting the process of counseling to the completion of counseling opens a discussion about hope, empowerment, and self-affirmation. By 'opening-to-close,' we assure the client that we have faith that this is a temporary setback and that the client will be able to manage daily struggles with personal power and insight.

▶ WHAT WORKS WELL

Much of the research on endings in therapy have oriented toward the termination-as-loss model. This model suggests a metaphor for ending the counseling process as a place for grieving through change, while acknowledging the growth in the process and the termination (Quintana, 1993). This model has provided a framework for a number of qualitative and grounded-theory approaches to evaluating counseling endings. Consistently, clients and helping professionals agree that endings that include client growth, outcomes, and changes resulting from the process, and the opportunity to say good-bye, typically result in positive transitions (Knox et al., 2011; Marx & Gelso, 1987). When clients initiated the counseling ending, satisfaction with the transition or termination was again related to accomplishment of counseling goals (Roe, Dekel, Harel, & Fennig, 2006).

Further exploration of the termination-as-loss model is ongoing, with critics suggesting an orientation toward consolidation rather than termination. Maples and Walker (2014) suggest that consolidation offers an active and strengths-based term for clients and helping professionals alike, wherein both parties are invited to integrate the counseling process into past and future self-concepts. These authors suggest that the importance of this language difference acknowledges endings in counseling as a transitional and collaborative natural phase.

This language has been adopted by other authors, who integrate a consolidation theme into transitional activities highlighting client change and relational closure (see Headley, Kautzman-East, Pusateri, & Kress, 2015). Further, consolidation has long been a theme of endings in the group setting, where clients are encouraged to integrate the relationships, new connections, and skills or insight from the group into their imagined future selves (Hudgins, 2013). Group members can also clarify what was witnessed in-session and what may be realistic after the transition (Jacobs, Schmmer, Masson, & Harvill, 2016).

▶ FUTURE RESEARCH

While endings will continue to frame the counseling process, it is necessary to grow the literature in collaborative, celebratory, and interactive approaches to this important transition. There are a number of member-influenced dialogues of creative and meaningful endings processes in public spheres (see Terry, 2011). However, counselors may still benefit from practical, theoretically grounded materials. In particular, the nature of the client concern may influence the utility of different ending strategies and discussions; there is currently very little research into how different initial concerns can influence the ending process.

There is also potential for further research into the impact of endings on the helping professional. In many cases, the ending of the therapeutic process is initiated by the client (Khazie, Rezaie, Shahdipour, & Weaver, 2016), which is understandably a difficult process for which to prepare. Further exploration of how premature endings affect helping professionals may prove valuable in decreasing professional fatigue and burnout. Interestingly, much of the current research in endings and transitions explores how to retain clients (Orcutt, 2013). As noted above, the satisfaction of the client in these cases is related to the accomplishment of counseling goals (Roe et al., 2006). However, more research is needed to see if these abrupt changes in therapy impact the client post-decision. This information may, in turn, influence how helping professionals frame client-driven endings.

Finally, there is a significant lack of information available about the cultural aspects of endings. It seems evident that different cultural experiences and backgrounds—both of the client and the helping professional—will influence the ending experience. However, questions remain about the influence of culture on the processing and celebrating of counseling transitions and endings.

Activities in This Chapter

Psychoeducational

Shifts (page 190): This activity invites clients to consider changes in future responses or behaviors that may result from changes in counseling.

Talk-Based/Motivational

Stop, Start, Continue (page 194): In this activity, the client identifies what they have stopped, started, and will continue as a consolidation of things learned or changes made from counseling.

Art-Based

Transformed (page 197): In this activity, the client is invited to visualize how they have changed by transforming colors and shapes into a new mosaic image

Relational

Celebration/Graduation (page 200): In this activity, the client is invited to explore other transitional celebrations using the metaphor of graduation to discuss transitioning from counseling.

Hands-On

Road of Life (page 203): In this activity, the client imagines the future from the moment after leaving counseling and explores what happens next, after this transition.

Group

Good-bye with Gratitude (page 206): This activity invites group members to bring sensitivity and gratitude to the group transition with a transitional letter of gratitude written by each group member.

▶ SHIFTS

AMOUNT OF TIME

20–40 minutes

MATERIALS NEEDED

- Pen/pencil
- Paper
- Summary of clinical notes (optional)

Type of Activity

Psychoeducational

Intent/Used for . . .

This activity invites the client to recognize specific strengths they have developed due to their work in previous sessions. Further, this activity invites the client to notice how activating these new insights or behaviors can influence their future experiences.

Step-by-Step Instructions

1. Begin the session by naming this as the final, graduating session. Inform the client that the purpose of today's session is not to begin any new therapeutic work, but rather to discuss the work that has progressed over the previous sessions. Let the client know that you have spent some time reviewing what has happened over time, and that you are interested to hear some of the client's thoughts about how they have changed since prior to the sessions.
2. If you are using a summary of clinical notes, share a copy with the client. If appropriate, expand on the brief summary by offering concrete examples of areas that the client changed or where insight has been evidenced in-session. Offering specific examples reaffirms the client's orientation to change and insight.
3. Invite the client to add anything that might be missing from the Outcomes and Future Steps. Use open-ended queries, some of which are suggested in the Guiding Questions section below.
4. Invite the client to recognize at least one change or insight that has resulted from attending counseling. This change might be as minor as attending sessions or conversing openly with the counselor. Explore, if appropriate, the change in client response that has resulted. Invite the client to deeply consider this shifted insight or change.
5. Affirm the client's response to these questions, acknowledging and complimenting the process while witnessing the work that has taken place.
6. Invite the client to consider situating this change or insight into their future actions. What are similar scenarios that the client might encounter where this change may be evidenced? If the client does not feel readiness to use these new skills anywhere outside of the helping setting, invite the client to simply 'pretend' by talking through a scenario where the skills might be applied.
7. Collaborate with the client, storying how these new skills, in this future anticipated event, may unfold. If the client becomes stuck, offer gentle reminders or suggestions of incidents that the client may have shared in-session, or that may have been witnessed in the counseling context. Continue to affirm and acknowledge the work and how these shifts or insights may influence the client in future interactions.
8. Discuss the client's readiness to apply the piece of work that has been explored in these sessions, including your personalized affirmation of the challenges of the work.

SUMMARY

Name H. Potter Counsellor AM Chilcote

Original presenting concerns: [what did client want from me?]

Transitioning into school, connecting with peers.

Manage relationship with adoptive family.

Duration, Frequency, Methods:

Six 55-minute sessions, weekly for first three sessions; bi-weekly for final three sessions.

Education, referral to school resources, art/expressive methods, communication skills.

Interpersonal exploration, life-story narrative and remembrance.

Outcomes [describe knowledge/changes based on participating in counseling]:

Psychoeducation/referral to school resources: tutoring, guidance, manual, athletics

Trigger identification, emotion regulation, communicating emotions, saying "no," saying "yes,"

Art/expressive methods for above.

Bibliotherapy- HP explored fiction related to managing grief and transition and chose "Elsewhere" by G. Zevin. Explorations of grief, influences on life, and legacy of his parents.

Future Steps:

Graduate from weekly counseling. Option for 1-3 check-in sessions before end-of-term.

Continue with team sports and chosen club, continue connecting with peers and peer support identified as helpful in session.

Self-refer to grief group if desired.

Figure 7.1 A concise summary allows the client to see the work they have done, while also opening a discussion and reflection on transitioning services.

Guiding Questions

- Looking back, these are some of the things that really stood out for me (list appropriate examples). If you imagine back to where you were when you started, and where you are now, what are some of the things that stand out for you?
- Do you notice any specific instances where you had an 'Aha!' moment? What are some of your landmarks or turning points along the way?
- How is this behavior, insight, or emotion different from how it may have been before counseling?
- What has made this change possible?
- Are you activating that new behavior, insight, or emotion in this moment, in this session? How?

Tips/Ways to Change

- Prior to the start of this session, you may want to review session notes from the start of the helping relationship and identify one or two areas of focus. Take some time to decide whether these changes can be documented for the client. Some agencies require a summary of notes as organizational policy, or for insurance purposes, and may have an internal document that serves this purpose. A cautionary note: care is to be taken with providing a translation of a clinical summary; the client should be informed of ways to protect the document should the client want the information to remain confidential. The client may not want to take the summary at the end of the session, but rather it may provide an in-session tool that is shredded after the session.
- The intention of this activity is to provide a brief summary of skills that have been practiced in-session. Inviting the client to acknowledge how something very small is transferrable to other areas of life is quite meaningful. If you are having difficulties describing any identified client change, return to the original concept: attending counseling or therapy. Did this happen? If yes, how is that different than before? Explore the steps necessary to schedule, arrive to, and participate in a session on the smallest scale possible. How might these small steps translate to other areas of the client's life?
- If part of the client's closing includes transferring to other helping services or accessing alternate community resources, this activity can be expanded to inviting the client to write their own goals for their future services. The client can take these goals with them into their first encounter to assist in verbalizing future changes.
- Consider how you would want to be affirmed for challenging and insightful work: Good job? Well done? Nice work? Consider integrating some of this into your language when moving through this activity.
- Even if some of the future thinking may seem like 'magical' or exaggerated thinking for the client, inviting them to visualize and talk through the use of skills reinforces the work and offers shifted future possibilities.

NOTES

▶ STOP, START, CONTINUE

AMOUNT OF TIME

20–40 minutes

MATERIALS NEEDED

- Paper
- Pen/markers
- Whiteboard (optional)
- Whiteboard markers (optional)

Type of Activity

Talk-based/Motivational

Intent/Used for . . .

This activity allows the client to verbalize some of the changes that have occurred during the counseling process and some of their personal characteristics that will persist and serve them in the future. Stop, Start, Continue focuses on specific actions that the client has taken, identifies behavior changes or insight, and allows the client to summarize their own work.

Step-by-Step Instructions

1. Begin the session by acknowledging and thanking the client for attending this final session. Inform the client that this session will not include any new therapeutic work, but rather will focus on summarizing the work that has occurred in previous sessions. Discuss with the client that the goal of today's session is to collaborate on a summary of the counseling work.
2. Use paper or a whiteboard and invite the client to create three columns. Label these three columns Stop, Start, and Continue.
3. Invite the client to describe the meaning of 'Stop.' Encourage the client to consider what aspects they might prefer to 'Stop' in terms of counseling, especially focusing on insight and behavior change. Refer to the Guiding Questions below if necessary.
4. Continue the activity with all columns, inviting the client to define and list 'Start' and 'Continue' behaviors in a similar manner.
5. Invite the client to add to some of the columns, sharing thoughts and discussion as they proceed. If the client has difficulty getting started, feel free to name 'Counseling' as both stopping and starting.
6. Continue affirming and validating what the client notices about their counseling process, encouraging the client to think of at least three things to write in each column—although more is fine.
7. If appropriate, ask the client if they would like your feedback or additions to the activity. If yes, choose a different color of pen to add one or two additional items in each column, if possible. Discuss these decisions with the client and ensure that the client affirms these observations. Some recommendations for responses are listed below in Tips/Ways to Change.
8. Review the entire list with the client. Invite the client to notice anything that stands out, or anything that is surprising. Encourage the client's reflection on the counseling process and what has been accomplished over time.
9. If appropriate and time allows, invite the client to choose one to three items that seem the most relevant to the process, and also to future behavior changes or insight for the client.

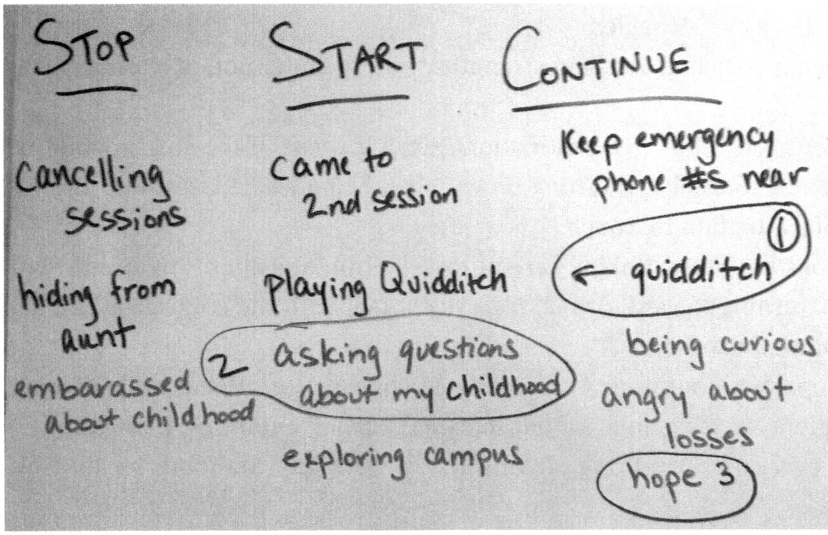

Figure 7.2 What were the client's hopes at the start of the process? By identifying specific movements that have been made, a client may celebrate the work that has happened in counseling.

10. Invite a discussion of how the client anticipates these actions will support them in the future. If time allows, explore this area with the client, allowing them to imagine a situation or scenario in which these skills or insights are enacted.
11. Validate and affirm the client's work across the counseling sessions and creation of the summary. Invite the client to take the summary that they created, or take a photo of the whiteboard image so that they might have an item of remembrance.

Guiding Questions

- When considering 'Stopping' in regard to changing behavior (or emotional response, or gaining insight), what are some of the things that people might want to 'Stop'? This might be different than everyday stopping.
- What are some things that people might want to 'Start'? And 'Continue'?
- Is it challenging to consider things that you would like to continue? Why or why not?
- How do you know that the continuing parts of yourself will be helpful?
- Which of these three columns feels the best for you?
- Can you rank these activities and share the top two or three most important for continuing on your therapeutic journey?

Tips/Ways to Change

- Prior to the start of this session, the counselor may want to review previous session notes and identify areas of insight or change for the client. This information may prove helpful should the client require additional prompting or practical examples.
- 'Counseling' may be included in all three columns. An offer of returning to counseling in the 'Continue' column reinforces that the client may access helping services in the future

and explores time in counseling as completing pieces of work rather than solving all of life's problems and struggles.

- I recommend focusing on client strengths, with the intention of closing and endings at the forefront.
- Suggestions for 'Stop': Procrastination. Staying silent. Canceling appointments. Staying closed to the counselor. Shutting down when being asked questions. Distracting myself. Not paying attention to myself.
- Suggestions for 'Start': Taking care of myself. Thinking about my health/well-being. Saying hello, turning toward, or making eye contact with the counselor. Finding the address of the counseling office.
- Suggestions for 'Continue': Counseling (if appropriate). Being open to suggestion. Asking questions. Getting angry about injustice. Feeling emotions. Expressing emotions. Not trusting everyone. Breathing. Taking five steps a day. Standing up for myself. Keeping myself safe.

NOTES

TRANSFORMED

Type of activity

Art-based

AMOUNT OF TIME

25–40 minutes

MATERIALS NEEDED

- Paper
- Glue
- Watercolor paints
- Brushes
- Oil pastels (optional)
- Chalk pastels (optional)

Intent/Used for . . .

This activity invites consideration of where the client was before counseling and how aspects of the client have been shifted or transformed. Clients are invited to choose colors to represent feelings or states prior to coming to counseling and recreate this image by tearing, modifying, and gluing to a new, transformed image. This activity invites a discussion around identified change and the challenges and surprises of an emerging, transformed self.

Step-by-Step Instructions

1. Acknowledge that this is the final session with the client. Inform the client that no new therapeutic concerns will be discussed today, and that the time will be spent creating an art image to signify the client's ongoing transformation as they move through the counseling process.
2. Invite the client to consider their initial state of being before or at the start of counseling. Encourage the client to consider mood, energy level, or social concerns as appropriate for presenting concerns and summarizing.
3. With these considerations in mind, invite the client to choose three or four colors that best represent the client's initial state at the start of counseling.
4. Instruct the client to use only lines and shapes to cover the entire sheet of paper with color, however they feel is appropriate, to illustrate their state prior to counseling. Encourage the client to complete this part of the art directive within five to seven minutes.
5. Invite the client to reflect on what they have represented (refer to the Guiding Questions below as needed).
6. Acknowledge the client's thoughtfulness about their state prior to coming to counseling, relating this reflective process to ending by looking back to see changes that may have occurred.
7. Instruct the client to tear the image that they have created into small pieces, trying not to crumple or destroy the paper if possible. This act sometimes requires encouragement, as the client may be attached to the image. When working with a client who is having difficulty tearing their created image, offer to take a photograph of the image and save it for them should they still want it at the end of the session.
8. Discuss transformation with the client. Acknowledging the work that the client has completed in counseling, discuss how transformation hints at growth as it entails using materials on-hand, shifting those materials to create something new.
9. Invite the client to transform their original presentation of colors and shapes into a new presentation. Offering a second piece of white paper, invite the client to glue the torn shapes together into a new image. If the client requests further direction or instruction, suggest to the client to organize the torn shapes into color or size, and imagine how these shapes and colors can be reorganized into a new image. Acknowledge the challenge of

Figure 7.3 While it might be challenging for the client to imagine how change can happen, this activity invites the client to create and move pieces of themselves into a new representation—a metaphor for change in counseling.

this activity, especially if the client was attached to their original image. Encourage and compliment the client's creativity and flexibility.

10. Offer the client seven to ten minutes to complete this transformed mosaic.
11. Invite the client's reflection on their transformed image. Discuss the challenges of tearing up something that was thoughtful and familiar, with the intent of turning this into something new. Expand on the discussion to include insights that the client may have regarding their own behavior changes, emotional changes, or insights that have occurred in the counseling setting.
12. Invite the client to discuss how they may experience this transformation after today. Discuss imagined encounters and encourage the client to anticipate how new skills or insight may be applied in these encounters.
13. Affirm and compliment the client's art piece and flexibility with the work and with counseling. Invite the client to keep their transformed art piece as a record of the work that they have done.

Guiding Questions

- What can you tell me about these colors?
- What is the significance of the lines and shapes in the original drawing? Are any colors mixed and, if yes, how does that fit for your emotional or social state?
- What do you notice when you look at these lines and shapes? What do you think is the most meaningful part?
- What was it like to tear up your original page with your original feelings or state of mind? Did you feel afraid? Relieved? Confused? Did any of these feelings mirror your feelings in counseling?
- How did you create your new image? Which parts were challenging and which parts came easily?
- What do you notice about this new image?
- How does this fit the work that you have been doing here? What does this have to do with ending today?

Tips/Ways to Change

- Discuss the offered materials with the client: watercolor paint, or oil or chalk pastels. The intention of these materials is twofold: first, these three materials are more fluid than other art materials and better offer opportunities for mixing and blending, fitting for a metaphor for emotional states. Second, these materials do not require lengthy drying or setting times, which is necessary for this activity.
- The use of metaphor can be useful throughout this activity. A metaphor for transformation could be the change from a caterpillar to a butterfly, or a seed to a tree.
- Sometimes I offer a larger piece of white paper for the transformed image and, if time allows, invite the client to use the remainder of the session to expand on the transformed image. This activity encourages discussion of future transformation, adding new materials and additional growth to create a more expansive image.
- If the client continues to struggle recreating an image to the extent that the session is not moving forward, suggest that the client organize the torn images into a contained circle. Use the Guiding Questions or your own questions to discuss containing feelings and states of being in a different way, and how this might influence the client's life in the future.
- If a client has created a previous piece of art as part of counseling that they have expressed they do not like or do not want to keep, you may invite the client to tear apart a previous art piece and recreate, with a similar discussion around transformation.
- If time is constrained or paints are unavailable, invite the client to choose from a selected few magazine images and, with the same instructions, tear the image into smaller pieces and reconfigure them into a different image.

NOTES

▶ CELEBRATION/GRADUATION

AMOUNT OF TIME

20–45 minutes

MATERIALS NEEDED

- Summary (optional)
- Certificate of Participation (optional)

Type of Activity

Relational

Intent/Used for . . .

This activity provides a metaphorical graduation for the client, wherein the counseling process is summarized for the client. There is an additional highlight of the counselor sharing how they have been changed or better informed by the client. The session discussion highlights other ceremonies that the client may have experienced and invites exploration of how completing counseling is similar and different, and how the client has changed since previous ceremonies.

Step-by-Step Instructions

1. Prior to the start of session, review client notes and consider if a documented summary is appropriate for the client (see figure 7.1 on page 191). Ensure that you, the counselor, are able to name at least one highlight of your time with the client.
2. At the start of the session, inform the client that no new therapeutic concerns will be discussed in this final session, but that the session is for reflecting on the shared time and influence of the client and counselor on each other.
3. Invite the client to reflect on any life events that included a ceremony, such as a graduation, wedding, birth, or cultural event (such as Quinceanera, Bat Mitzvah, etc.). Encourage the client to consider the actions and activities leading up to this event. Explore things such as

CERTIFICATE Of PARTICIPATION

H. Potter

is thanked for his outstanding participation and his commencement

PRESENTED BY: AM Chilcote

ON THIS DAY: May 19, 2016

Figure 7.4 A Certificate of Participation is a fitting ceremonial exchange that works well in the counseling setting to signify an ending.

who was involved, the meaning that the client made of the event, and how the client felt during and after the ceremony.

4. Acknowledge the combination of excitement and responsibility that sometimes comes with graduating and crossing the metaphorical threshold.
5. Share with the client one or two of their characteristics that stand out. This may be a meaningful time to share a memorable interaction with the client, where the client influenced you, caused you to pause or reconsider an idea, or collaborated in such a way that it uniquely influenced your interactions in another sphere.
6. Offer the client an overview of the summary of therapeutic work, if desired. Invite the client to reflect on the summary or add/change any particular items, as described in Shifts (page 190).
7. Acknowledge and congratulate the client on counseling graduation. Offer the client the Certificate of Participation, if desired.

Guiding Questions

- Why do you think we have traditional ceremonies for life changes? How are we changed by crossing that stage—real or metaphorical?
- If you could have a graduation ceremony from counseling, with a gown and a stage and a big celebration, who would you invite? What would that ceremony look like?
- How has this relationship (client–helping professional) influenced other relationships? Or, how is it different from other relationships?
- What is it like to know that you have graduated from these services?
- How is graduating from counseling different from endings in other relationships or areas of your life?

Tips/Ways to Change

- Some of the relational approaches described here will not be right for all practitioners, nor for all clients. If your client does not present with a relational style in-session, or you do not feel that the relationship is flexible to the extent that the client would be helped by any self-disclosure, use caution with this activity.
- Consider discussing the importance of ceremonial endings in your own tradition, if this fits for your relationship with the client. There can be benefits to using self-disclosure with intention; however, again be sure to reflect on the therapeutic relationship before doing so.
- If appropriate, this is the best session in which to provide the client a cupcake.
- Many common word-processing programs have templates for certificates (such as the one pictured). There are a number of alternate certificates available, or you can modify this activity toward an art directive and invite the client to create a certificate of graduation of their own design.
- My office includes a small, brightly colored basket filled with envelopes. These envelopes include brief notes of encouragement, and clients are encouraged to take one/leave one as necessary. A meaningful addition to this graduation session could include inviting the client to write a note of encouragement for someone who might need it and to leave it in the basket.

NOTES

▶ ROAD OF LIFE

Type of Activity

Hands-on

AMOUNT OF TIME

20–40 minutes

Intent/Used for . . .

This activity invites the client to consider the metaphor of a Road of Life to visualize and anticipate future actions and events. This activity is oriented to the future, the continuity of the client, and comfort with leaving the counseling setting.

MATERIALS NEEDED

- Paper
- Pen
- Whiteboard (optional)
- Whiteboard markers (optional)

Step-by-Step Instructions

1. Begin the session by discussing with the client that no new therapeutic issues will be discussed today, but rather today is meant for considering what will happen for the client after today. Offer the client time, if appropriate, to discuss how this session may feel different from previous sessions. Acknowledge that this might be a difficult shift for the client and affirm the client's ongoing participation in today's session.
2. Invite the client to consider the metaphor of the 'Road of Life.' Use the Guiding Questions, or your own questions, to encourage the client to connect with this metaphor.
3. Using paper and pen, or a whiteboard, invite the client to draw a point on the piece of paper that will signify their leaving the session today. Then, invite the client to draw a line that will signify the road that they will take when they leave here. Encourage the client to be as creative as desired—this road may simply include the rest of the day, the week, or farther into the client's life.
4. Invite the client to include any road signs, stops, or landmarks along the route that they may anticipate. Begin with experience-near events, such as the client having dinner at the end of the day, and expand from there.
5. As time and interest allow, affirm the client's additions and encourage more, if appropriate.
6. Review the Road of Life with the client, complimenting their connection and participation in the activity. Invite the client to reflect on imagining the future beginning a few moments from now and how this influences their thoughts or feelings.
7. Invite the client to reflect on any moments that they might be looking forward to, or moments that the client hopes to avoid by taking an alternate road.
8. If appropriate, invite the client to place any flag-posts along the Road of Life where the client would consider returning to counseling or seeking helping services from the community.
9. Acknowledge future challenges and celebrations that the client might encounter and the collaborative work that was done in the counseling setting. Compliment and affirm the client's closing, inviting them to keep the Road of Life with them as a map of the future.

Guiding Questions

- Do you know of any stories, movies, or songs where a road is a main setting? Why do you think a road provides a good setting for a story?
- What are some of the roads that you take regularly? Are there times when you have had to make an unexpected turn or change direction? What was that like for you?

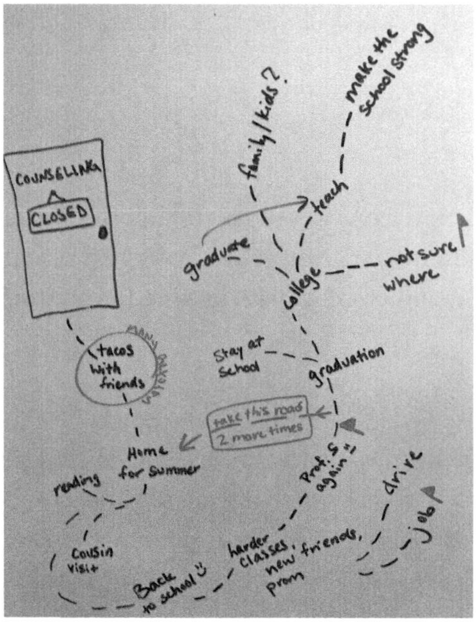

Figure 7.5 What does the imagined future hold—both near and far? Connecting with small, yet significant, moments in daily life, such as 'tacos with friends,' invites imagining small next-steps after the conclusion of counseling.

- How do you know when a road really works for you? And when it doesn't?
- What are your thoughts about the road that you have created here today?
- If this road that you have created included some of the landmarks you have encountered while in counseling, which ones would you highlight?
- How does this fit with the theme of today being the last session?
- What are your plans after you leave the office today? Do you believe that you will be different in any way?

Tips/Ways to Change

- This activity can be expanded to a complete art activity by offering art materials and inviting the client to fully illustrate their future Road of Life.
- Expanding this activity might include identifying resources or tools that the client may have developed in the counseling process to navigate the Road of Life.

NOTES

Endings

GOOD-BYE WITH GRATITUDE

AMOUNT OF TIME

20–40 minutes

MATERIALS NEEDED

- Paper
- Pen/markers
- Stationary
- Postcards (optional)
- Envelopes (optional)

Type of Activity

Group

Intent/Used for . . .

This activity is intended to allow group participants to write down closing thoughts or words regarding their group experience. This activity is useful in generating a conversation of gratitude and respect for time spent together, and also offers clients a transitional object to take away from the group—a note of gratitude.

Step-by-Step Instructions

1. Prior to the start of the final group session, group facilitators should discuss and decide whether the final session will include any additional therapeutic or skills work beyond ending or transitioning. This discussion may also include group members, if appropriate.
2. At the start of the group session, acknowledge and compliment attendees for arriving at the final session and inform the group that some time will be taken during the group to discuss endings.
3. Invite the group to recall their hopes or intentions when beginning the group. Invite members to explore what their expectations of self and others may have been at the start, and what they have seen throughout the group process. Continue this conversation, encouraging group members to share, until you observe a natural transition point for the conversation.
4. Thank the group members for participating in the group, acknowledging the challenges of group work versus individual work, especially the need for trust in relationships when moving through the therapeutic or skill work.
5. If appropriate, share one or two of your reflections of your own observations of the group process—for instance, how the inter-group dynamics changed over time, or ways that the group held space for each other during challenging moments.
6. Acknowledge that there are some in the group who may be looking forward to the group ending, and some who might be feeling anxious or sad about the group ending. Invite all group members to pause for a moment to determine their personal position on the ending.
7. Acknowledge that group members may encounter each other in the future, either in the community or in future groups, and that this group process will have changed relationships between group participants beyond what their relationship may be with others. Affirm that the group experience is memorable, with the sharing of both comfortable and uncomfortable experiences.
8. Invite each group member to choose stationary and a writing tool, and with these reflections in mind, to create a closing message of gratitude to either the self or another group member. Inform the group members that this paper will be passed around the group so

Some days it was just about getting through the session and sitting still, and you made it.

I didn't expect to laugh so much.

Thank you for listening and sharing.

I will probably see you again because we go to the same school, and now when I see you in the hallway and we make eye contact it will be like I KNOW YOU and YOU KNOW ME.

Even if I don't see you again, I will remember that we were here together.

Seeing someone who is going through the same things as me makes me feel less alone.

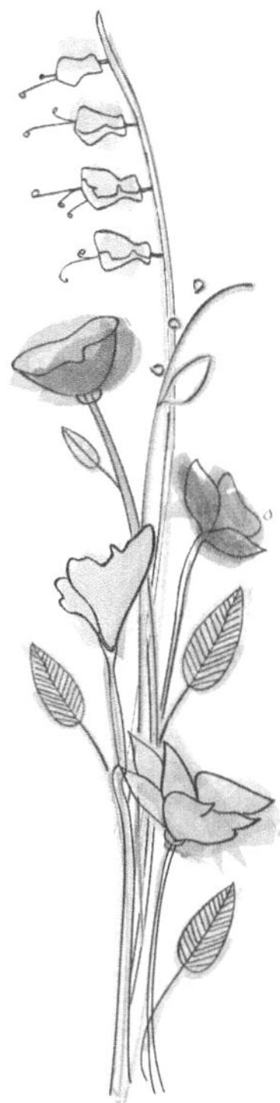

Figure 7.6 This group activity affirms the work of both the individual group member and the influence of the relationships (a). It also offers the participant a transitional object to recall group members and thus, group content (b).

that the group member may write accordingly. Encourage members to write one or two sentences on the paper, leaving space for others.

9. Allow about two minutes for writing, and invite group members to pass their card to the next person. Invite group members to sit for a moment, again, and reflect on their experience before continuing writing. Encourage group members to write an additional note of gratitude or sensitivity before continuing with passing the note.
10. When the group is halfway done with the act of writing and passing notes, encourage the group members to pause and consider future encounters with group members, and what those experiences may feel like. Acknowledge, again, how group members will have different relationships than before, as they know each other in ways that others do not. While this might feel a little uncomfortable for some, this is a profound and connecting trust. Invite group members to consider this reality and continue writing.
11. Continue passing the notes until each group member has received their original note. You may invite group members to read their note, if time allows. Offer envelopes if group members would like to contain this good-bye with gratitude.
12. Thank the group members for attending and participating in sessions and for participating in today's final group activity. The facilitators should take their time with this final thank you before ending the session.

Guiding Questions

- Did today feel any different to any of you in coming to this group, knowing this is the final session? How is this the same or different than our previous meetings? The first day?
- How was this group what you expected? How was it not what you expected?
- Is your intention for your participation the same today as it was when you started the group?
- How has this experience been memorable?
- Were there times when you thought you would not be able to complete the group? How did you get through it?
- Endings can be challenging, and sometimes we may prefer to just walk away without facing the good-bye. How are you with today's ending?
- Is there anything about today's goodbye that contains elements of a future hello?

Tips/Ways to Change

- Ahead of the session, decide whether to orient the entire group session toward this topic or simply the last 20 minutes of the session.
- Group members may be invited to place completed notes in a basket and draw a note out randomly, rather than keep the note that they started.
- An alternate, but equally meaningful, integration of letter writing for group members is to invite group members to write a note of affirmation and encouragement to the self, acknowledging the work that has been done in the group, and then to write a second note to an 'unknown' group member. The second note is placed in a basket and passed around, where group members will then have two notes of encouragement, gratitude, and affirmation.
- A level of literacy is required for this activity, and counselors should be sensitive to the various reading and writing levels of group participants. Illiteracy and other language barriers are very challenging and well-hidden concerns of many adults. An alternate suggestion for a shared gratitude experience might include adapting Give a Gift, Get a Gift (page 56), integrating language of endings.

▶ OTHER RESOURCES

Baum, N. (2007). Therapists' responses to treatment termination: An inquiry into the variables that contribute to therapists' experiences. *Journal of Clinical Social Work, 35*, 97–106. http//:dx.doi.org/10.1007/s10615-006-0066-0

Howes, R. (2014). Terminating therapy. *Psychology Today*. https://www.psychologytoday.com/blog/in-therapy/201406/terminating-therapy-part-v-therapist-termination

O'Donohue, W. T. & Cucciare, M. A. (2008). *Terminating psychotherapy: A clinician's guide*. New York, NY: Routledge.

Zeig, J. K. & Gilligan, S. G. (Eds.). (1990). *Brief therapy: Myths, methods, and metaphors*. New York, NY: Brunner/Mazel Inc.

▶ REFERENCES

Headley, J. A., Kautzman-East, M., Pusateri, C. G., & Kress, V. E. (2015). Making the intangible tangible: Using expressive art during termination to co-construct meaning. *Journal of Creativity in Mental Health, 10*(1), 89–99. http://dx.doi.org/10.1080/15401383.2014.938185

Hudgins, L. (2013). Closing time: Clients' shared experiences of termination of a music therapy group in community mental health. *Qualitative Inquiries in Music Therapy, 8*, 51–78. Retrieved June 1st, 2016 from http://www.barcelonapublishers.com/resources/QIMTV8/QIMT8-3_Hudgins.pdf

Jacobs, E., Schmmer, C. J., Masson, R. L., & Harvill, R. L. (Eds.). (2016). *Group counseling: Strategies and skills* (8th ed.). Boston, MA: Cengage Learning.

Khazie, H., Rezaie, L., Shahdipour, N., & Weaver, P. (2016). Exploration of the reasons for dropping out of psychotherapy: A qualitative study. *Evaluation and Program Planning, 56*, 23–30. http://dx.doi.org/10.1016/j.evalprogplan.2016.03.002

Knox, S., Adrians, N., Everson, E., Hess, S., Hill, C., & Crook-Lyon, C. (2011). Clients perspectives on therapy termination. *Psychotherapy Research, 21*(2), 154–167. http://dx.doi.org/10.1080/10503307.2010.534509

Maples, J. L. & Walker, R. L. (2014). Consolidation rather than termination: Rethinking how psychologists label and conceptualize the final phase of psychological treatment. *Professional Psychology: Research and Practice, 45*(2), 104–110. http://dx.doi.org/10.1037/a0036250

Marx, J. A & Gelso, C. J. (1987). Termination of individual counseling in a university counseling center. *Journal of Counseling Psychology, 34*(1), 3–9. http://dx.doi.org/10.1037/0022-0167.34.1.3

Orcutt, M. (2013). *When clients leave therapy: Premature termination from the client's perspective.* (Doctoral dissertation). Retrieved from Proquest.com. (Publication Number 3610229).

Owen, J., Smith, A., & Rodolfa, E. (2009). Clients' expected number of counseling sessions, treatment effectiveness, and termination status: Using empirical evidence to inform session limit policies. *Journal of College Student Psychotherapy, 23*(2), 118–134. http://dx.doi.org/10.1080/87568220902743660

Quintana, S. M. (1993). Toward an expanded and updated conceptualization of termination: Implications for short-term, individual psychotherapy. *Professional Psychology: Research and Practice, 24*(4), 426–432. http://dx.doi.org/10.1037/0735-7028.24.4.426

Roe, D., Dekel, R., Harel, G., & Fennig, S. (2006). Clients reasons for terminating psychotherapy: A quantitative and qualitative inquiry. *Psychology and Psychotherapy: Theory, Research, and Practice, 29*, 529–538. Retrieved June 1st, 2016 from http://www.ncbi.nlm.nih.gov/pubmed/17312869

Terry, L. (2011). Semi-structured termination exercises: A compilation from the groups in college counseling centers listserv. *APA Divisions: Group Psychotherapy Column-The Group Psychologist.* Retrieved May 21st, 2016 from http://www.apadivisions.org/division-49/publications/newsletter/group-psychologist/2011/04/termination-exercises.aspx

Afterword: Hope-Work

When I started out as a counseling student, the idea of giving clients homework seemed like such a silly notion. I can still remember two distinct thoughts: "Why would I ever want to use CBT?" (I had some issues with the CBT framework when I first began in this field, and thought homework was for CBT only), and, "Why would clients even want to do homework? That's why they'll be paying me the big bucks—to give them the answers!" (I was obviously misguided regarding the role of a counselor, as well as how much money we make . . .).

Over the years since then, I, like many helping professionals, have realized that I was wrong about many of my ideas I had when beginning my training. For me, one of those shifts developed around my views on homework. It started when I was, again like many counselors, invited to participate as a 'client' for some newer trainees. I cannot remember the specific topic that I brought forth, but I do remember that when the allotted time was up, the counselor-in-training stood up and said, "Okay, well I will see you again in a week!" Though the session itself had been great, I left feeling like something was missing. Over the following years, through my own experience and practice, I recognized that many clients are looking for a 'takeaway,' or something that can tide them over until the following session. In fact, I have worked with some clients for whom the whole experience is considered worthless unless they are able to come away from it with something practical, or at least something that will get them thinking.

Homework, when given effectively, can lead to a wealth of growth and development, both between sessions and even lifelong, after the final session. For both Autumn Marie and me one of the intents of counseling should always be to encourage reflection and self-empowerment, which is certainly a possibility when the client is given appropriate homework. Regardless of whether a client actually completes a homework or not (I let clients know that counseling homework is always optional), the effect from simply thinking about homework can be impactful.

Of course, there is typically a point at which you realize homework is only effective when it is applicable and relevant to the client—and it can be difficult work finding that 'perfect' homework. Throughout this book, there are a number of topic-specific homeworks that can certainly be useful and adapted to a number of situations outside of their given context.

However, sometimes you are looking for a homework that isn't particularly specific to one given topic, something that, quite simply, can *give hope*—regardless of the client's issue. In this section, Autumn Marie and I have compiled a list of some of our favorite homeworks—short activities and thought experiments that can provide a practical goal between sessions while ideally sparking some hope along the way. As with everything in this book, please take what you will and adapt as you desire. Enjoy!

Freeman

▶ HOPE-WORK

- Each day, think about what your top self-oriented goal will be (embodying a trait for a day).
- Plan to make one person smile the next day, before/as you're going to bed.
- If you had a magic wand that could grant only one wish, and it had to be a 'selfish' one, what would you wish for (must wish for something, *not* for something to disappear).
- Let yourself fail.
- Let yourself feel.
- Find a song that best represents how you currently feel. Then find a song that best represents how you would like to feel.
- Come up with a *different* name (i.e., not anxiety, depression, etc.) for what you are experiencing, one that reflects for you what it is.
- When you get home (or to your room), look around the space. Let your eyes settle on one thing in your space. Notice what your attention is drawn to.
- Notice three (or five) things in your personal space that are your favorite color(s).
- Imagine you are a ninja warrior of peace and compassion. In a safe space, throw a few silly ninja punches or high kicks, and imagine that with each punch or kick, that peace and compassion enters the room. Smile, because this is very silly, and I just made it up right now.
- For 30 seconds, try walking very slowly and deliberately. Very slowly, notice how nearly all of your muscles are engaged and working with just this one step. Very slowly and deliberately, notice how one foot touches the floor as one foot leaves the floor.
- Place your hand on the back of your neck, your cheek, or your chest for a count of 12. You probably do this a number of times throughout the day, but this time, only do this. Notice any temperature difference between your hand and your body during this count of 12. Without trying to make any meaning of this, just notice what you actually feel.
- Pick one person that you see through the day that you feel neutral toward—maybe someone you don't know who is waiting for the bus, or the person driving the car that passes you, or someone you see outside walking the dog, or someone like the postal worker that you might not see. In your mind (or aloud if it is reasonable), wish for that person a day full of positive experiences and happiness.
- Look up a motivational quote or song lyric that you like and bring it in for the next day.
- Each night before you go to bed, think about one thing you will tell yourself at the same time the next night.
- For one conversation every day, allow yourself to listen, and only listen, without feeling the need to respond/think of 'the right thing to say.'
- Go for a walk, drink some water, and eat more broccoli.
- When you wake up each morning, ask yourself what your five-year-old self would want you to do today. As you're going to bed, ask yourself what your five-year-old self would find the most incredible about what you did today.
- If you could have a superpower, but weren't allowed to use it for helping (or hindering) others, what power would you want, and how would you use it?
- Design a t-shirt with your personal motto on it.

Afterword: Words We Like

Throughout my training as a counselor, I have experienced moments when hearing the language of another therapist has been incredibly helpful. This often comes through peer review or consult and supervision, but sometimes the language of the experts, such as Michael White or Insoo Kim Berg, are very specific, relatable, and credible. Hearing this language and integrating it into my own practice continues to be a critical part of my development as a counselor. While I have my personal commonalities as a therapist—questions that I like to ask or that reflect my personal style—I also appreciate alternate language. I would be willing to suppose that clients appreciate this as well, as many of us have heard or seen the stereotypical question: "how does that make you feel?"

I do not take my ability to communicate effectively for granted, and I should not. Oral communication is often misunderstood, misguided, inaccurate, and sometimes just completely confusing. In a therapeutic setting, relationships are delicate, and words are a very powerful tool when used toward problem resolution. Encouraging a person to share information that would be helpful toward a reduction of symptoms, or to help the therapist better understand the situation, is a challenge that every helping professional encounters, and often knowing how to ask a question in multiple ways supports movement in-session.

The following are a few phrases or questions that the authors have found useful in therapy. We find these words facilitate discussions toward exploring and discussing emerging themes for the client and directions in counseling. You will notice that these might be stylistically different for you, and that is okay. Try using a few, and if they do not feel like they fit your language or relational style in-session, try integrating some of the language with your personal style.

For any helping professional, it is always important to consider:

> What are some of the key words and phrases you use in a counseling session?
> What do those words and phrases say about you?

Autumn Marie

WORDS WE LIKE

- What else? Tell me more about that.
- What is the one thing you are most likely to remember from this conversation? What is one thing you would most like *me* to remember?
- How would your friends/family describe you? Can you give me an example of why they would describe you that way?
- What aspects of 'the problem' work for you? What parts do you want or need to keep?
- What parts of you do you hold onto while you work through this? What practices are grounding?
- What are the parts of you that don't like this problem?
- When you describe that situation/problem, I feel it right in my heart (or gut). What is it like for *you*?
- How does this story/incident/memory connect with some of the other things we have been exploring?
- What do you feel is right for you, in your heart?
- Who else wants you to be here today? Does that matter?
- What went well for you today?
- Who are your allies in this? [or] Who else gets what you are going through?
- Who/what brings out the best in you? What are you like then?
- When all of the 'stuff' around this settles, what do you think is at the heart of the matter?
- [Silence. I like to count to seven in my mind.]
- That's so much. Which of those issues is the most pressing/distressing for you right now?
- Wow. How *have* you been surviving?
- That sounds so clinical (depression, anxiety, etc.); I'm wondering if there's a name you could give this that better reflects your own experience?
- Let's just sit with that for a moment.
- Thanks so much for sharing that with me. How was that for you?

Index

For Product Safety Concerns and Information please contact our EU representative GPSR@taylorandfrancis.com Taylor & Francis Verlag GmbH, Kaufingerstraße 24, 80331 München, Germany

Batch number: 10731490

Printed by Printforce, the Netherlands